The Future of Law and Economics

The Future of Law and Economics

Essays in Reform and Recollection

GUIDO CALABRESI

Yale UNIVERSITY PRESS

New Haven and London

Yale University Press books may be purchased in quantity for
educational, business, or promotional use. For information,
please e-mail sales.press@yale.edu (U.S. office)
or sales@yaleup.co.uk (U.K. office).

Set in Minion type by IDS Infotech, Ltd.
Printed and bound by CPI Group (UK) Ltd, Croydon, CR0 4YY

ISBN 978-0-300-23052-9 (pbk)
Library of Congress Control number: 2015940941

A catalogue record for this book is available from the British Library.

10 9 8 7 6 5 4 3 2 1

To Kate, Sam, Adam, and Ginevra, who are the future

Contents

Preface

This book has been long in coming. As its subtitle suggests, it represents ideas that I have, for many years, been pondering over. As such, different parts, in different ways, have been the subject of seminars, workshops, and lectures in any number of places. There are too many to recognize individually here. But if a reader sees something in the book and remembers a discussion about it in his or her school, I mean today to let that reader know that I too probably remember and am grateful.

There are, however, some more proximate helpers who must be mentioned. Robert Post, the dean of the Yale Law School, has been unfailing in his support, and so have my colleagues at that school. These friends, both in a recent workshop and individually, have been more than generous in their criticisms, suggestions, and encouragement. That they continue to treat this sometime scholar and oft-time judge as one of their own means more to me than I can say.

John Donohue and the American Law and Economics Association, and Alain Marciano and Giovanni B. Ramello, also deserve special note. The first awarded me the Coase Medal and thereby led me to pull together the thoughts that underlie the last two chapters of this book, to which, incidentally, both John Donohue and my colleague and friend Bruce Ackerman made particular contributions. The second organized a conference titled "Law and Economics: The Legacy of Guido Calabresi," published in 77 Journal of Law and Contemporary Problems 2 (2014), which led to the structuring of the ideas which are the core of what, here, is chapter 6.

A book like this could never have been written were it not for the patience and help of my longtime assistant Susan Lucibelli. Her name properly appears in all but one of my books, as she and I have been working together for more years than can decently be said. My law clerks past—Cat Itaya, Luke Norris, David Wishnick—and present—Nate Cullerton, Eric Fish, Kevin Lamb—deserve special mention. They have been tireless in their editing, footnoting, and bluebooking, and they did all this without a whimper on top of all their work on my judicial cases and opinions. It is a joy to have people around me like them and my other assistant Marge Greenblatt. Finally, and as always, my deepest thanks go to my wife, Anne, who for more than fifty-four years has been my loving companion, wisest critic, and dearest friend.

One more thing needs to be said. This book is not a "scholarly" book in the ordinary sense. It does not purport to canvas the literature or to recognize all or most who have written on the various topics that I discuss. That is what I was inclined to do when I was a full-time scholar and teacher. My reluctance to deviate from that mode, together with the fact that I do not have the time to undertake that level of research while also being a judge, explains the long delay in this book's "coming." Many people, however, have urged me to put into writing, before dotage sets in, ideas that have been percolating in my mind for years. The result is this book. To the extent that the book fails to give proper recognition to scholars who have preceded me with respect to some of the things I here write, I apologize, and I hope that, as a result of this book, their own scholarship may become better known even outside of their own particular fields. I say this in general, but especially as to those practitioners of Welfare Economics who, I do not doubt, have foreshadowed me, but whose work has, unfortunately, not been much noticed by those other practitioners to whom this book is distinctly addressed, the Lawyer-Economists. It is some of these who, in my judgment, on too many occasions proffer criticisms of the existing legal world on the basis of economic theory that does not, without more, justify that criticism.

The Future of Law and Economics

I

Of Law and Economics and Economic Analysis of Law
The Role of the Lawyer

When John Stuart Mill was asked who were the seminal minds of the century (probably 1750–1850), he gave two names: perhaps surprisingly the poet Samuel Taylor Coleridge and, of course, Jeremy Bentham. Of Bentham, Mill said that he approached all ideas as a stranger and if they did not fit his test (the test of utility), he dismissed them as vague generalities. Mill then went on to say that what Bentham didn't realize was that "these generalities contained the whole unanalyzed experience of the human race."[1]

In my way of defining the terms, Bentham can be viewed as the paradigmatic Economic Analyst of Law, while Mill's approach is the precursor of that which characterizes Law and Economics.[2] In this introductory essay I will explain what I think the difference between Law and Economics and Economic

Analysis of Law is, and why Mill and Bentham exemplify each. I will then give examples of recent scholarship of both sorts and where they fit historically. Finally, in this essay I will discuss why *legal* scholars have a particularly important role to play in Law and Economics, and especially in its future. All this will be a kind of introduction to seven essays that will follow and form the core of this book. In these I will use a Law and Economics approach to consider (1), (2), and (3) what we mean by merit goods—and why economic theory needs to accommodate two very different types of such goods; (4) the perdurance and proper analysis of altruism and of not-for-profit institutions—and what that implies for economic theory; (5) what the use of the liability rule, in practice, tells us of the relationship between markets and command; (6) what economics, while denying it is doing so, often says about the validity of various tastes and values, and why it does this; and (7) what economics can properly, and very usefully, say about the shaping of tastes and values.

A.

What I call Economic Analysis of Law uses economic theory to analyze the legal world. It examines that world from the standpoint of economic theory and, as a result of that examination, confirms, casts doubt upon, and often seeks reform of legal reality. In effect, it acts as an Archimedean place to stand and upon which to place a lever, a lever that permits the scholar, when appropriate, to argue for change in that legal reality. In its most aggressive and reformist mode, having looked at the world from the standpoint of economic theory, if it finds that the legal world does not fit, it proclaims that world to be "irrational." And this, of course, is exactly what Bentham did when he tested laws and behavior on the basis of utilitarianism and, in his most aggressive moments, dismissed what did not fit as nonsense or, indeed, "nonsense upon stilts."[3]

What I call Law and Economics instead begins with an agnostic acceptance of the world as it is, as the lawyer describes it to be. It then looks to whether economic theory can explain that world, that reality. And if it cannot, rather than automatically dismissing that world as irrational, it asks two questions.

The first is, are the legal scholars who are describing the legal reality looking at the world as it really is? Or is there something in their way of seeing the world that has led them to mischaracterize that reality? This question is what Melamed and I were led to ask by our article now commonly known as "The Cathedral."[4]

The simple economic model we there developed suggested that there should be situations in which the law permitted the victims of a "nuisance" to abate the nuisance but required those "victims" to pay damages to the nuisancor, that is, to compensate the nuisancor for the harm that abatement caused him. Yet there seemed to be no such cases in the legal literature.[5] Rather than dismissing the legal reality as irrational, however, we looked at that reality more carefully. It quickly became apparent that, for good reasons rooted in the limited capacities of courts, virtually no *appellate-court cases* would exist to which this "reverse damage rule" could be applied. And it was at that limited, appellate-court reality that nuisance law scholars were looking. If, instead, one properly expanded the legal world to consider administrative decision making, the "world" would be seen to be full of instances in which "reverse damages" existed.[6] In other words, economic theory had served to lead legal scholars to a more accurate, more comprehensive view of legal reality.

If, however, even a more comprehensive view of legal reality discloses rules and practices that economic theory cannot explain, Law and Economics asks the second question. Can economic theory be amplified, can it be made broader or more subtle (without thereby losing those characteristics that give it coherence and make it as powerful as it is) so that it can explain why the real world of law is as it is? If such a more nuanced theory can do this, Law and Economics then proposes that this expanded economic theory be used more broadly. It suggests that the changes imposed on economic theory to make it capable of explaining a specific legal reality be made part of economic theory generally.

In a sense, that is what the founders of what has come to be called behavioral economics brilliantly did with respect to a series of issues. Observations of behavior, made principally by very sophisticated empirical psychologists, demonstrated behavior that traditional economic theory could not explain.[7] The data were powerful and extremely well documented. Rather than ignoring this behavior or dismissing it as irrational or inexplicable, as for a considerable time many traditional economists had done, behavioral economists used the data to bring about changes in economics itself. And then, not surprisingly, indeed as I am suggesting almost inevitably, the changed theory has been used to examine and successfully explain other areas (including, notably, many legal interrelationships) that previously had not answered to or been understood by a simple Economic Analysis of Law.[8]

To my way of thinking, then, behavioral economics is a particularly significant instance of the kind of bilateral relationship between economic theory and the world as it is that I am here urging more generally under the name of Law and Economics. Behavioral economics derives from a variety of different empirical sources (not solely or even primarily from lawyers), but it has much in common with, and indeed can be viewed as an especially important example of, the kind of analysis I am here discussing.[9]

Indeed, if one looks again and with a slightly different eye at *Tragic Choices*, a book that Philip Bobbitt and I wrote in 1978, one finds analysis there of much the same sort.[10] To pick just one example, the discussion in that book of the "sufficiency paradox" might, if written today, be viewed as a paradigmatic example of behavioral-economics scholarship.[11] As we there explained, the paradox consists in the willingness of society to spend much more to save a person in dramatic peril than to avoid recurrent disasters that kill far more people, precisely because doing so serves to assert the "pricelessness of life," and because not doing so would dramatically negate that priceless-ness, especially in the face of so many other decisions that, al-beit less conspicuously, price life in ways that we find morally repugnant.[12]

My point is not to claim that *Tragic Choices* was an early—and hence, at the time it was published, perplexing—precursor of today's behavioral economics.[13] Rather it is to say that what I am asserting here is a generalization drawn from work done by many others, myself included, in the recent as well as the more distant past.

B.

Of course, there will be times when even an expanded economic theory will not be able to explain legal reality. The lawyer-economists may then give way to some other "Law and . . ." discipline and see if the legal world can be justified or even only explained on the basis of theories or experiences that cannot be incorporated into economics without causing eco-nomics to lose its coherence and force. This too can be seen in behavioral economics' occasional yielding to psychology and in *Tragic Choices'* sometimes explicit appeal to anthropology for help.[14] And there may even be times when a combination of various disciplines, including economics, will be needed to explain the world as it actually is.[15]

There will also be times, moreover, when the lawyer-economist—recognizing, as Mill himself did, that legal reality does not by any means always represent worthy human experience but may instead reflect outdated or otherwise undesirable rules—will become as harsh a critic of the legal reality as Bentham was and, like Bentham, become the fierce proponent of *radical* reform.[16]

In this sense, while in Economic Analysis of Law economics dominates and law is its subject of analysis and criticism, in Law and Economics the relationship is bilateral. Economic theory examines law, but not infrequently this examination leads to changes in economic theory rather than to changes in law or in the way legal reality is described.

This is, I think, what Mill had in mind when he criticized Bentham. It was not that the whole unanalyzed experience of the human race was necessarily good. It might represent centuries of exploitation, mistaken ideas, or approaches that new technologies rendered obsolete. Analysis (and, to Mill, utilitarian analysis) remained necessary to ferret these out. But, as Mill made clear, that unanalyzed experience might also, and crucially, shed light on gaps and flaws in the *theory* that Bentham sought to apply. The world of human experience must—bilaterally—be both the subject of theoretically based analysis and criticism and the source of corrections and amplification in the analyzing theory.

One further point needs to be made before I turn to the history of Economic Analysis of Law and of Law and Economics and discuss a few of the leading practitioners of each. When considering Economic Analysis of Law it is important to remember that the "top-down" examination of the legal world that characterizes it does not imply *any particular* economic theory. To Bentham, the analysis of the real world and his proposed reforms flowed from his application of straight utilitarianism. To many modern practitioners of Economic Analysis of Law, the theory is "Chicago" or "Viennese." But precisely the same approach could use Marxist economic theory. In each case there is a "chosen" theory; the legal world is examined through the prism of that theory; and if the world does not fit it is dismissed, anathematized even, and, the practitioner hopes, replaced by a reality that fits the chosen theory.

The same capacity to employ any of many economic theories applies also to Law and Economics. The theory that is amplified to make it explain and respond to the actual legal world can be Marxist economics, pure utilitarianism, Vienna transplanted to the Windy City, or Keynes redux in New Haven. It is not the *theory* used that distinguishes the approaches. The theory can vary. It is, rather, the relationship between the theory and the world it examines that separates them.

Indeed, the same relationship may apply more generally between the canons of *any* scholarly theory and the legal world that such a theory seeks to explain, describe, and criticize. Thus, it applies as much to modern philosophy, when *it* seeks to explain the legal world, as it did to Bentham's utilitarianism and does to economics today.[17]

In this book I will, however, limit myself to the relationship between economic theories and legal reality. And it is to examples of the difference between Economic Analysis of Law and Law and Economics and to where these examples fit historically that I now turn.

C.

To understand the modern importance of both Economic Analysis of Law and Law and Economics, one must go back to the early part of the twentieth century. At that time—as I, among others, have written—many legal scholars were chafing at the restraints that the then-dominant view of law was placing on them. Law was canonically seen as an independent discipline. The values that the legal system furthered were an inherent and seemingly not to be questioned part of that system. Where they came from and how they had become part of law was rarely examined. The job of the legal scholar was just to make law more consistent with itself, and significant reform was not the legal scholar's purview. Interstitial work to achieve greater consistency and explication of the logical interrelations of the system was what legal scholarship should be about.[18]

This had not always been so, of course, and Bentham stands out as the mightiest of those who earlier had not accepted such a tyranny of the past. Nor was the canonical approach dominant in all the law schools of the United States. At Yale, for some odd historical reasons, a different approach governed even then.[19] This was typified by the fact that the father of modern sociology, William Graham Sumner, taught economics at the Yale Law School at the end of the nineteenth century and was only one of several non-law teachers who were part of the Yale Law faculty at that time. Nevertheless, at the end of the nineteenth century the dominant American (as well as European) view was that law was independent of other disciplines and properly formalistic. The Yale approach was an aberration.

All this began to change in America early in the twentieth century. Scholars like Roscoe Pound of the Harvard Law School refused to accept a legal world in which past legal structures governed and could only be changed either by revolution (*Écrasez l'infâme*, throw out the old, and establish a whole new legal world) or by unanalyzed majoritarianism (whatever the majority wants is best). Such scholars saw the job of scholarship in general and legal scholarship in particular—as Bentham had—to be an important means of criticizing and improving the legal world. This meant that radical legal reform—rather than either acceptance of the past or of revolution—could be argued for by legal scholars. It also meant that what the majority seemed to want at any given moment was itself to be made the subject of analysis and criticism. To this endeavor Pound enlisted the young and already quite remarkable Arthur Corbin of Yale Law School. Pound then managed to get Corbin and Yale to recruit Wesley Hohfeld (after apparently failing to have Harvard do the same).[20]

But what was the basis of the legal reform that Pound and the others sought? How could one change the law without a point external to law—a source of values separate from law—on which an Archimedean lever could be placed that would be used to move the law? To Pound that place lay in the social sciences; to others it could be found in philosophy.[21] More generally, it was the basis of all the "Law and . . ." movements—each of which sought by looking outside of law to find a way of altering law and making it better. I have elsewhere discussed these various approaches and what they had in common with each other. Their differences from each other—while crucially important as to the reforms and results they might favor—were, I argued, small in regard to their approach to law generally and especially so in comparison to their differences from the classical legal-formalistic viewpoint they were attacking.[22]

At this point, though, there was no clearly defined difference between those who—as Bentham had done—simply analyzed and criticized the existing legal system on the basis of whatever outside discipline or disciplines they chose to use and those who—as Mill had suggested—employed the outside disciplines in a bilateral relationship with the legal order. In my terms, there was no clearly established distinction between lawyer-economists and economic analysts of law.

In this respect, Arthur Corbin's farewell letter to the Yale Law School faculty, which to my knowledge has not been formally published and which I attach to this book as an appendix, is a source of particular insight. In this letter, written, I believe, in 1941 when he reached retirement age (but, as it happened, before he did some of his most significant scholarship), Corbin, perhaps looking back on the enthusiasms of his youth, warned of too ready a reliance on extralegal disciplines as a source of truth and, by implication, of legal reform. He had been, let us remember, an early adherent of "Law and . . ." approaches and of extralegal Archimedean points from which the legal world might be moved and reformed. And he continued to be one in the great works he was still to write.[23] But in this letter he made clear that simple reliance on such outside, social science sources of values was as flawed as reliance on the preexisting formal legal structure. In essence, the great Arthur Corbin, like Mill, was—to return to my terminology—warning against a simple use of Economic Analysis of Law and implicitly citing the need for the bilateral relationship that Law and Economics exemplifies. Use the outside discipline, he seemed to be saying, but if it fails to explain the legal world don't reject that world out of hand; see, instead, if that world can lead to a deeper, more articulated outside discipline.

D.

Who, then, became the twentieth century's major practitioners of Economic Analysis of Law and who of Law and Economics? The greatest example of the second was, of course, not a lawyer at all; it was Ronald Coase. He was, however, one of an odd breed of economists that for much of the twentieth century dwelt on the fringes of core economic theory, an institutionalist. I will soon enough suggest why I think *lawyer-economists* are, on the whole, more suited to the job of doing Law and Economics than latter-day institutional economists. But, in truth, modern Law and Economics must begin precisely with Coase, the institutionalist.

In his great early article "The Nature of the Firm," Coase asked the prototypical Law and Economics question.[24] If, as economic theory of the time posited, markets were costless, there would be no firms. Relationships would be entirely market and contractual. But firms did exist. Why? Rather than ignoring that existence or treating it as somehow irrational, Coase made that *datum* from the world as it is the basis for a change in economic theory. Would it destroy or make that theory impractical to have it treat markets as having costs that could then be compared with the costs of nonmarket command structures like those that characterized firms? Of course not.[25] Considering the costs of markets not only made available an explanation of the existence of firms and of many of the legal structures that their existence entailed, but also altered economic theory for the better. And in due course this change became the basis for economic theory's ability to explain any number of other things it previously had not been able to cope with.

This was especially so after Coase published his parallel article, "The Problem of Social Cost," which, among other things, considered the implications of the costs both of markets and of command more broadly.[26] The capacity of markets to limit the effect of so-called externalities and of markets and command structures to reduce the costs of each other are but two examples. As it happened, another early-twentieth-century institutional economist, Walton Hamilton, was crucial to the first writings of the other person whom Richard Posner credits along with Coase as the founder of the mid-twentieth-century "new" Law and Economics, myself.[27] Hamilton, like the early Coase, was not overly welcomed in economics faculties and so became a professor at the Yale Law School. There, he combined with Harry Shulman to put together some materials on Torts. He soon abandoned that field, concentrating instead on antitrust, the field of law that economics more traditionally tilled. Indeed, after he retired, he actually became a lawyer, joining some of his distinguished students, Thurman Arnold, Abe Fortas, and Paul Porter, to practice antitrust law in their celebrated firm in Washington, D.C. But his early stamp on the torts materials remained.

In time Fleming James, a great legal scholar, but one who, even more than Harry Shulman, had only the most limited economics training, updated the Hamilton-Shulman torts materials. By the time I came to Yale Law School these materials had been published—under Shulman's and James's names.[28] It was that casebook that James used, in 1955, when he taught me torts. That casebook, in paradigmatic Law and Economics fashion, examined the world of real cases and, again and again, implicitly looking toward economics, asked for explanations of why the law was what it was. Sometimes the answer lay easily in classical economic theory; sometimes it did not, but could be readily found there: if economic theory were only altered and amplified a bit!

I think it is fair to say that it was that posing of questions, which as a student I attempted to answer, that led to my first article, "Some Thoughts on Risk Distribution and the Law of Torts."[29] The article was first drafted in 1956–57 as my "competition piece" for an officership in the *Yale Law Journal* very shortly after I had finished Torts with Fleming James. The article reflected my good fortune in having earlier had, as tutors in economics, three subsequent Nobel Prize winners—James Tobin at Yale and Lawrence Klein and Sir John Hicks at Oxford—and as classroom teachers at Yale, two extraordinary economists—Warren Nutter (who later became a founder of the Virginia School of Economics, in which Coase found an early American home, and who showed me the power of the classical Chicago approach) and William Fellner (who represented the best and most subtle of the Viennese take on welfare economic theory). But the article was also a response to the fundamental Law and Economics questions that Walton Hamilton had put into what had become the Shulman and James casebook. What is the world of law, and can economic theory explain it? And when it cannot, is the problem that the legal rules are outmoded, irrational, the product of now-overcome relationships or even of past exploitations? Or can these legal rules be explained, and indeed be seen to make very good sense, if economic theory were altered and amplified?

My article was published contemporaneously with Coase's greater "Problem of Social Cost."[30] And, along with Coase's piece, it became the source of a ten-year period of quite remarkable flourishing of Law and Economics. That period has, unfortunately, been somewhat overlooked.[31] And it is worth remembering at least a couple of those whose amplification of economics and law, in the light of Coase's and my early scholarship, was especially fruitful. Wally Blum and Harry Kalven come immediately to mind because their friendly polemic with me, in the years right after the publication of my first article, represented how a Law and Economics approach could push the quest further in both fields.[32] But Harold Demsetz should be mentioned most of all. He was the economist who, in my judgment, used Coase's insights most immediately and successfully to amplify economic theory and to use that broader theory to explain crucially important legal phenomena such as the creation of property rights and the role of liability rules in torts.[33] His work remains for me among the very finest examples of Law and Economics scholarship done by an economist in response to work of both lawyers and economists.

What is especially interesting about this period is that much of the work being done then *was* Law and Economics and not simply Economic Analysis of Law. Of course, at the time, the prevailing economic theory did explain any number of previously problematic-seeming legal phenomena quite adequately. It did so without need of alterations or modifications. The discussion of the doctrine of *respondeat superior* in my first article is an example.[34] It could certainly be described as simple Economic Analysis of Law. But what also characterized these early pieces was the constant back and forth between the two disciplines and the rarity of the Bentham-like approach; the rarity of a viewpoint that said, "Let us test the world in the light of the theory and if it is wanting, say so, period!"—a statement that, in my terminology, defines Economic Analysis of Law. When did this latter approach enter the picture and why has it become so central, so dominant even, today?

The answer lies in the extraordinary achievements of an extraordinary person, Richard Posner.

In 1970 I published my book *The Costs of Accidents*. It collected and went beyond several earlier essays.[35] Its publication marked, I think, the end of that first period of "new" Law and Economics scholarship. There were several reviews of the book. One by Frank Michelman opened up a totally new road in Law and Economics scholarship.[36] It led, in time, to "Property Rules, Liability Rules, and Inalienability: One View of the Cathedral" (with A. Douglas Melamed) and the huge literature—typical Law and Economics—that followed it.[37] But—as important as Michelman's review and the road it opened was and continues to be—another review, by Richard Posner, was at least as significant.[38] It was the beginning of Posner's transformation of Law and Economics into Economic Analysis of Law.

In lecture after lecture, article after article, and book after book, Posner demonstrated how powerful an *existing* economic theory can be when it is used to test, confirm, and cast doubt upon the world of law.[39] With Benthamite genius and prodigiousness, Posner began systematically to look at all of the world of law in light of economic theory. That the theory Posner used is one associated with Chicago is no accident given that what first drew him to economics was that very Aaron Director who, on the Chicago Law faculty, first published Coase and who played a significant role in my being offered a full professorship there, in 1960, even before Coase joined that faculty.[40] But in the end this reliance on Chicago theory is less important than is Posner's single-minded use of *an existing* economic theory to test the world. I believe Posner actually coined the term "Economic Analysis of Law." But whether he did or not, and whether he consciously changed the focus from Law and Economics to Economic Analysis of Law as a description of what was and should be done, is ultimately less significant than what happened.

Following on Posner, an immense amount of Economic Analysis of Law scholarship has been published. Its achievements should not be underestimated. The whole reconception of antitrust law that occurred in the latter part of the twentieth century in response to that scholarly approach is a dramatic example of its power and effectiveness.[41] But that is just one instance. In fact, field after field of law has been analyzed—and, not infrequently, changed—because an economic analysis of that field led to the conclusion that the preexisting world was, if not quite "nonsense upon stilts," at least of dubious rationality.[42]

I stand in awe of this. Hence, my aim in this book is neither to limit nor to criticize Economic Analysis of Law. In the past, I have at times done a fair amount of it myself (while suggesting its dangers).[43] And it is certainly true that Bentham and Posner have achieved great things. For, it is worth emphasizing once more, the world as it is represents not only Mill's unanalyzed experience of the human race but also, as Mill fully recognized, centuries of exploitation, surpassed rules, and no longer desirable relationships.[44] And the Posners and Benthams have helped us to see and overcome many of these.

But the world as it is often also represents worthy relationships and behaviors that the theory—as it canonically is—does not explain. And it is essential—whether under the rubric of Mill's utilitarianism, of Coase's institutionalism, of behavioral economics, of *Tragic Choices*, or of Law and Economics—that such data from the world as it is be used to reform the theory. It is essential to do this both (a) because what the empiricist describes is often not irrational but highly worthy and should not only be retained but also explained, and (b) because the reformed theory becomes a far more useful tool for doing Posnerian reform in the future.

For these reasons, my aim here is to demonstrate the importance—indeed, the necessity—of the *other* approach: Law *and* Economics. It is to show, in the essays that follow, *its* utility for both disciplines.

In doing this I want to be clear that recognition of the difference in these two ways of looking at economics and law and at their relationship to each other is neither new nor especially original with me. I have noted it in passing in quite a few lectures in the past.[45] And, some thirty-five years ago, I had occasion to read the syllabus for the basic welfare economics course at Cambridge University. (Alas, I do not remember what teacher/professor had put it together.) It assigned readings of works by Posner and by me. And it said that the difference between us was that Posner used economic theory to criticize and correct law, while Calabresi, though he did that too, more importantly *also* used law to suggest changes and alterations in economic theory. The person who wrote that syllabus thus succinctly and independently described the distinction between Economic Analysis of Law and what I call Law and Economics.

E.

One thing remains to be mentioned before I turn to the substantive part of this book. Why—if what I am describing is so general a lateral relationship between empirical and theoretical work—am I emphasizing Law and Economics in this book? And, even if I limit the theoretical side to *economic* theory, why do I focus on legal scholars as the source of real world data rather than, say, institutional economists like Coase and Hamilton? The reason is itself historical-empirical.

In theory, there is no reason why the bilateral relationship should concern itself principally with economic theory and with law. The back and forth I've talked about can be well nigh universal. But as a practical matter, if one is talking about reforming society and its rules today, one most often begins with law and with dominant legal relationships. It is no accident that

Bentham was, almost more than anything else, a prodigious legal reformer. And the success of Economic Analysis of Law tells us the same thing. True, Pound and the legal reformers of the early twentieth century did not view economics as the only (or perhaps even the principal) Archimedean place to stand on to change the legal world. They had hoped that other social sciences would be as helpful. And certainly historical, philosophical, psychological, anthropological, theological, and literary analyses have been and should be used for the same purpose. But it remains a fact that none of these have, in practice, been as effective in the Benthamite task as has economics. Not surprisingly, Posner himself has explained why he believes this to be the case.[46] And, whatever the reason, I think it is hard to dispute the significance of economic theory to the Benthamite mission.

That, however, leaves open the question of why it should be the legal scholar who represents the other side in the bilateral relationship that I describe as Law and Economics. Why should it be the legal scholar, rather than an institutionalist, who presses economic theory to reform and amplify itself? The reason is twofold. First, and most obviously, if the relationships and structures that economic theory is being used to reform are legal ones—as they seemingly so often are and have been— the legal scholar is likely to have an understanding of those structures which is both easier and deeper than that of other empiricists viewing them. It should be easier for the legal scholar to look at what economics is analyzing and to say, "valid, unanalyzed experience of the human race" or "pretty likely surpassed and timeworn," than for a scholar from a discipline other than law. Of course, an outside view has its advantages and can give insights too, but for the run-of-the-mine cases the lawyer-economist should be able to react to the insights and criticisms of economic theory most readily, and hence should be the one most able to take the next step in the bilateral relationship I have been discussing.[47]

There is, moreover, an additional historical reason why I believe the legal scholar has a particularly important role to play. This derives—for whatever reason—from the peculiar relationship between institutional economists and economic theorists. Were it not for this troubled relationship, which I will discuss shortly, one might well say—yes, of course, lawyers have an advantage over psychologists or whatevers, since, in this context, *law* is what economic theory is analyzing. But why should the *empirical* reaction come from legal scholars rather than from economists themselves? Why look to lawyers? Should we not rather try to clone Coase?

In theory, there is no ready answer to that question. In practice, though, the reason why so much of Law and Economics scholarship has been done by lawyers, with Coase being the great, great exception, is clear. Institutional economists have, too often, been described by economic theorists as having an axe to grind, usually an ideological one.[48] As such, the empirical responses of institutionalists to what the economic theorists have criticized in law have—at times correctly, but often also too readily—been set aside as based not on facts describing legal structures that people (for perhaps unanalyzed reasons) actually desire, but on ideological longings for a world of the institutionalists' own desire. To the extent that institutionalists—including Coase himself, when he wrote "The Nature of the Firm"—can be set aside in this way, as representing a particular ideology instead of being "honest" fact observers, the bilateral relationship is severely weakened.[49]

Lawyers, instead—unlike economists—are necessarily empirical. We cannot avoid being institutionalists. We are trained, from the start, to look at *cases*, at relationships, at real-world situations. That is one important thing that—especially in the common law, casuistic tradition—we do. The universality of lawyers' institutionalism means that lawyers, as institutionalists, come in every ideological stripe. One can no more, *ex ante*, criticize a legal scholar's criticism of an economic theory's *pronunciamento* of "irrationality" as being ideologically based than one can, today, say the same of the subsequently libertarian Coase's "Nature of the Firm."[50]

Sometimes, however, as I said earlier, the same case-relatedness that makes lawyers good institutionalists can keep legal scholars from correctly perceiving what the actual world looks like. And this fact is worth reemphasizing here. If one looks only at cases, and perhaps primarily only at appellate cases, real-world relationships that for some reason do not find their way into those cases can be missed. And then, in a proper Law and Economics bilateral relationship, economic theory, through its model building, can lead legal scholars to reexamine the real world and see legal structures that they had missed. This, let me repeat, is what happened in the now-famous case of the fourth rule in nuisance law. The right to abate a nuisance, but only if the abater paid the nuisance damages, for very good reasons almost never found its way into an ordinary appellate case.[51] A simple economic model suggested that such a rule should be there. And when lawyers looked more carefully, they found that it was, in fact, applied all the time ... administratively. Economic modeling led legal scholars to see the real world more clearly![52] This example, however, precisely because it demonstrates how the bilateral relationship between the economic theorists and legal scholars can help legal scholars understand the legal world better, underscores the utility of having such *legal* scholars play the institutionalist role. It in no way reduces their centrality.

To summarize: The lawyer, the legal scholar, has a special, and especially crucial, role in the bilateral relationship that Law and Economics scholarship involves. This is because it is *law* and legal institutions that are the subject of that scholarship. It is also because the legal scholars' part in that bilateral relationship is played by legal scholars of every sort of ideological persuasion.

But, let me be careful. I am not for a moment suggesting that this is the sole or even the most important role that legal scholars should play. Law is an immensely rich and complex field. What are and what should be legal rules must, I believe, be looked at in any number of different ways by any number of differently guided legal scholars. As I have suggested repeatedly, and wrote explicitly in my article "Four Approaches to Law," Law and Economics is just one of many "Law and . . ." approaches. And "Law and . . ." approaches are only one set of many extraordinarily fruitful and important ways of doing legal scholarship.[53] Claude Monet made at least as many paintings of haystacks as he did of the Cathedral at Rouen. If law is as much a haystack, full both of hay and of needles to be found, as it is a cathedral, the role of the lawyer in Law and Economics scholarship that I discuss in this book represents only one view of the haystack. It nonetheless remains a particularly powerful depiction.

F.

It is with this background in mind that I now turn to the core of this book and talk about six areas in which Law and Economics scholarship seems to me to be most promising and needed. What will derive from these essays—from this examination of the *real* legal world—will be the suggested amplification of economic theory to take account of six things:

  a. the significance of what may be called "interpersonal utility effects" or "third-party moral costs" to the proper treatment of widely different goods and bads;

  b. the existence and utility of the interplay of nontraditional or semi-markets and of nontraditional or decentralized command structures to the proper allocation of goods and bads in many areas;

  c. the importance of the fact that many goods and bads are both means to achieve a *desideratum* and *desiderata* (ends), in themselves, and that, indeed, markets and command *themselves* represent the same duality;

  d. a more nuanced recognition of the relationship between command and market structures in wide parts of the law;

  e. the actual—and unavoidable—existence of value judgments underlying much economic analysis; and

  f. the capacity of economic analysis, under quite traditional economic theory assumptions, to give guidance as to the desirability of a variety of tastes and values.

In all this, and as to each of these things, I wish to be quite clear. I do not for a moment suggest that economists and economic theorists have failed to consider them in the past. The literature of economics and economic theory is rich beyond words, and distinguished scholars have deeply discussed these and many more issues beyond those considered in this book. My quarrel, if it is one, is rather with Economic Analysis of Law.

For all too often its practitioners, whether economists or lawyers, have reached conclusions as to the desirability of existing legal structures that ignore the above-mentioned issues, and in this way have failed to push canonical economic theory more regularly to expand its models to respond to these "real-world" data.

II

Of Merit Goods
Commodification and Commandification

A. Merit Goods Defined

Many years ago, Richard Musgrave at Harvard and James Tobin at Yale called attention to the existence of groups of goods that our society (and most other societies as well) does not allow to be allocated in the way the preponderance of goods are.[1] They called these goods merit goods, and sometimes styled them as goods that respond to merit wants. They then stated that what characterized these goods was the fact that decisions as to their purchase and uses did not adequately take into account their costs (or benefits) to others in society. They wrote that there were goods (and bads) as to which individual market decisions do not adequately take into account the external benefits and costs that result from their production and use.[2]

All that is fair enough, but in the end that definition is not terribly helpful. Individual decisions with respect to any number of goods create externalities—positive or negative. And, as Coase demonstrated, the market itself operates (within the limits of transaction costs) to reduce or eliminate such externalities.[3] Moreover, while most goods and bads create external effects, when one looks at those goods and bads that in the world of law one seems to be speaking of when one speaks of merit goods, one sees that the externalities associated with such goods are different from the run-of-the-mine externalities that economic theory has long dealt with.

It is true that your decision not to keep up your house may impose costs on me, your neighbor. And these costs are not simply the decline in the market value of my house from its being next to a rundown dump. Such other costs that you impose may involve, for example, the greater danger of fire to my place from the fact that your home is inadequately maintained. Yet, I would argue, it is not these ordinary sorts of externalities—externalities that are now adequately analyzed in economic theory—that might possibly lead people to speak of housing as a good different from ordinary goods. It is not these traditional economic externalities that could perhaps cause us to attach the Musgrave/Tobin terminology to housing, and might lead us to call it a merit good.[4]

What, then, *are* merit goods (and bads) in our society, what is it about them that makes them different from other goods (and bads), and what does a focus on them imply for economic theory? Or, to put it another way, to echo the *leitmotif* of this book: (a) what are the particular and special externalities that attach to some goods and bads that seem to define them—in the real world—as different from most goods and bads; (b) what does recognition of these externalities and these goods and bads require of economic theory if it is to explain their almost universal existence; and (c) how would the development of such an amplified economic theory make it more capable of dealing with, explaining, and perhaps reforming other legal relationships and structures?

I believe that what are appropriately termed merit goods come in two types. Some are goods that a significant number of people do not wish to have "priced." That is, to put it in a more traditional way, they are goods whose pricing, in and of itself, causes a diminution in utility for a significant group of people. They are "pearls beyond price"—at least we would ideally like to view them as such—whose commodification is *in itself* costly.[5] But other goods, to which the term "merit" is appropriately applied, are goods whose pricing is not intrinsically negative. They are goods whose bearing a market price is not, *in itself,* costly, but whose allocation through the prevailing distribution of wealth is *highly* undesirable to a significant number of people. It is not their pricing that is objected to by many; it is the capacity of the rich to outbid the poor that renders their allocation through the ordinary market unacceptable, utility diminishing, and therefore "costly" to many people.

There is undoubtedly much overlap between these two types of merit goods and bads. That is, there are some the very pricing of which causes significant external costs, *and* whose allocation (whether through a pricing system or otherwise) in response to wealth differences leads to large external utility diminutions as well. But there are also many goods, as I hope to show soon enough, to which only one of the two sources of external costs above described predominantly applies. As a result, the analyses and possible treatment of these two different categories of merit goods are best done separately. Both differ from the generality of goods whose market allocations lead to more traditional sorts of external costs (e.g., the housing-fire example mentioned earlier). Some of these traditional externality-causing goods may, of course, overlap with one or both of the two types of merit goods I have just pointed to. But the difference in the sort of external costs these traditional goods cause, from the kinds that attach to what I am calling merit goods, makes analyzing them together unhelpful. There is, moreover, a significant sense in which the two categories of merit goods I have noted are similar to each other, *and* different from ordinary goods whose allocation also causes external costs. And that similarity is both worth underscoring and discussing. The external costs that the goods *I* call merit goods cause are *mental sufferings* that their allocation in the ordinary market imposes on other people. The external costs attributable to these goods, when they are priced or allocated through the ordinary market, are the pain other people feel because they do not like that kind of pricing allocation. In that respect, they have more in common with moral costs than with more immediately economic costs. But that does not make them less real or less needful of attention. Nor, for reasons I will mention in due course, can economic theory ignore the reality of such external moral costs if it wishes to explain the world of actual legal relationships.

My objection to your doing something that I deem to be immoral—whether it is knowing that you are doing something I abhor far away from me, or seeing you doing it in public (think of any number of sexual antics that some object to)—is no less real and costly to me than the pain I feel if you punch me in the face. No less a lawyer-economist than Robert Bork pointed this out long ago.[6] A society may choose, as Mill perhaps urged,[7] to ignore or override some or all of these "moral" costs, for good or bad reasons,[8] as it can choose to override or ignore any number of more traditional costs. But, again, this does not make them at all less real. And economists (assertedly dedicated to the proposition that tastes and values are outside their field of competence) can least of any one ignore them.[9]

The costs that adhere to merit goods are moral costs. But they are not direct moral costs. They are more complex than the costs ordinarily dealt with in economics, because they represent not only what classically were called externalities, but what are also only moral externalities. That too, however, does not make them less real or significant. The pain I suffer from having an exact price put on "life" *is* real. And so is the pain I suffer if I see the rich buying body parts that pretty much only the poor sell. Whether I am wise or foolish in these respects is, at this stage of the analysis, neither here nor there. What is important, though, is that these indirect external moral costs are far more difficult to internalize through Coasean transactions than are traditional externalities. Indeed, as to these costs, Coasean internalization is almost always impossible. And equally significant is the fact that collective/command ways of internalizing these sorts of externalities are also extremely problematic.[10] That means, without a doubt, that analysis and treatment of these external costs is hard and that integrating their reality into economic theory is no easy task.[11] But these difficulties in no way lessen the reality of these costs, or their impact on the legal order that we actually see, and hence on the need to find—hopefully in economics—a way of examining them. An economic theory that includes and deals with these costs, with these moral externalities, can help us discern whether the legal order that has grown up in response to their existence is nonsense (upon stilts, perhaps), is a quite good response, or is a fair response, but one that—guided by economics—can be bettered and reformed, to society's benefit.

Once we abandon the impermissible value judgments that would, *ex ante*, deny weight to these particular types of costs, economics can move quite readily to developing ways of considering how best they can be dealt with in different societies. Musgrave and Tobin presciently told us about the existence of merit goods. But they left us all a lot to do in deciding how best to handle them. It is to taking a few halting steps in that direction that I now turn. To do so, however, requires a separate examination of the two categories I posited: (a) goods that many do not want to have priced at all, that many do not want commodified, and (b) goods whose commodification would not really bother us, if only their allocation, the market for them, were not determined by the wealth distribution that prevails generally.[12]

B. Commodification and Commandification

Life is a pearl beyond price, and yet we trade it off all the time. Not surprisingly, scholars spend considerable time and effort in trying to figure out what is the appropriate value to put on life in a variety of circumstances, so that good decisions may be made as to when and how much it is worth spending to save it, and when not.[13] Indeed, many years ago, in the early days of the new Law and Economics movement, I wrote an article with an intentionally provocative title, "The Decision for Accidents," which argued that our society and our system of tort law frequently decide that some accidents and their harms are worth having, since it costs too much to avoid them.[14] Soon after, the *New York Times* ran an editorial pontificating that when safety was at stake no amount of money spent was too great.[15] I was tempted, for a moment, to write a letter expressing my delight at the editorial and looking forward, thereafter, to having no *New York Times* delivery trucks run faster than, say, five miles an hour (in order to avoid road accidents). But I quickly thought the better of it.

I realized that though what I wrote—that we in fact (in some sense) decide all the time that many accidents are worth having—was right, it was also true that (in another no less fundamental sense) we want to hold on to, and assert, the ideal that life is beyond price. Paradoxically, therefore, the *New York Times* was also perhaps speaking truthfully. Moreover, this paradox, which Philip Bobbitt and I explored more fully in our book *Tragic Choices*,[16] expresses itself dramatically in our reluctance, disgust even, at any actual *pricing* of life. In order to adhere to the ideal that the *New York Times* was speaking to, we avoid "commodifying" life; we refuse, as much as we can, to price it.[17]

Life, however, is in this respect just one of a series of goods that, to a greater or lesser extent, share the characteristic I have been describing. As to all these goods, putting a market price on them is something that is *itself* costly. Life is the paradigmatic example, but it is, in fact, only one of many goods whose too obvious pricing is painful to many in our society. It is this category of merit goods that I wish now briefly to discuss. I will spend less time on it—important though it is—than on the second category of merit goods, because it has already been the object of my concern and treatment, albeit in a somewhat unsystematic fashion, in both my torts articles and in *Tragic Choices*.

If, as is the case, there is a category of goods that we do not wish to price—because pricing is costly—but to which we do not actually give absolute value since, in fact, we trade such goods off against other *desiderata* (whether money, convenience, or great ideals, like equality)[18] all the time, how do we manage the trade-off? The essence of these merit goods is that *pricing* them is costly. It is not that they are absolutes. How then do we decide how many of them we want, for whom, and when? What do we substitute for a market price in making that decision if, by hypothesis, it is the pricing of them that is costly? The answer would seem obvious, but, in fact, it is not. If pricing is too costly, why not substitute command? If what we dislike is the *commodification* of these idealized goods, then why not use the other, traditional, decision making process of economic analysis and allocate them through a collectively arrived at command decision? Instead of using the market to decide who gets to live and who doesn't—or to determine how worthwhile it is to give up other *desiderata* to protect the lives of individuals—let us just make that decision collectively and order the result. The trade-off between the pearl beyond price and what, in fact, we want as badly is then achieved by regulation and not by the market.

The problem with this approach—quite apart from whether we believe such collective decisions can reflect individual desires as ably as markets can, or at least can adequately take such individual desires into account—is that the very societal attitudes that make *pricing* such goods costly also make their too-obvious trade-off by regulation and command *painful.* If we do not want to *price* lives (and we don't), we also do not want the government to tell us, too obviously, that some lives, in some circumstances, are not worth saving. Commodification of some goods is very costly, but so is its non-price alternative, *commandification!*

Examples of this are legion. The amount we spend to save those who try to row across oceans and get into trouble, and the obsession with hostages taken and with "saving them," are but two relatively common instances of avoiding—at great monetary cost—the *moral cost* of collectively trading off lives. These and others are discussed at length in *Tragic Choices.*[19] But one example is worth repeating because it helps us understand how, in fact, our society seeks to deal with this category of merit goods. When the Pentagon Papers case was being argued before the Supreme Court, Justice Stewart asked a troublesome question of Alex Bickel, the Yale professor who was arguing for the *New York Times* against the imposition of any "prior restraint" against the publication of the "secret" Pentagon Vietnam materials. Justice Stewart asked, "Let us assume that when the members of the Court go back and open up this sealed record, we find something there that absolutely convinces us that its disclosure would result in the sentencing to death of a hundred young men whose only offense had been that they were 19 years old and had low draft numbers, what should we do?" Bickel answered, in effect, that that was not the case before the Court, so the Justices should not worry about that hypothetical now. And Justice Stewart, in his opinion allowing publication, followed that advice.[20]

Justice Black, whose opinion in the case was his last, said, I am told, "The question was the right one, but the answer given was not." The problem in Black's view was *not* that one hundred lives would be lost. A hundred lives are lost all the time for all sorts of good, bad, or indifferent reasons. To Black, a hundred lives to protect freedom of the press was, *in fact,* a cheap trade-off. The problem was that, in the context posed by Justice Stewart's question, there would be *a judicial sentencing to death* of that one hundred. There would be a decision at the highest level of our state that these one hundred lives were not worth saving. There would, in my locution, be a *commandification* of the worst sort. Such extremely costly commandification had to be avoided.

The answer, Black suggested to his clerks, rather brutally perhaps, was that a legal structure was needed so that, in any actual life-taking case, the lives would be lost without the need for any approval by our Highest Court. It was that *focused approval* that was unacceptably costly, not the life–press freedom trade-off. And that focused trade-off could be avoided, he believed, by a generalized rule against any prior restraint of such publications, if such a rule were established in a case in which lives were not, in fact, at stake. The result would be that, when those lives *were* taken in a case that actually did involve lives, the taking would occur without any focused High Court decision and approval. Accordingly, the costs of commandification would be significantly reduced. Leaving aside whether the great absolutist Hugo Black was right or wrong in the particular case, his approach and Potter Stewart's questions are central to an understanding of how this category of merit goods is, in fact, dealt with in our society.

The first thing to notice is that it is pure markets and pure command that are most costly. Modified markets and modified command (à la Hugo Black) may achieve the desired trade-offs with lower (or perhaps even no) moral costs than those incurred if pure pricing or clear command are used. (And I'll have much more to say about the incorporation of modified markets and commands into economic theory when, in a later essay in this book, I discuss altruism.) The second thing to notice is that not all merit goods in this category necessarily give rise to the same, or even equivalent, costs of pricing and command. As to some, the allocation/trade-offs achieved by putting a clear price is especially costly, while even a clear command does not give rise to much disgust. As to others, the opposite is true. Direct governmental decision may be especially noxious, while even a fairly obvious price might not.

When one of these allocation methods is distinctly less objectionable (less morally costly) than the other, we naturally gravitate to, and use predominantly, the pure approach that is less costly. I say "gravitate to" because an interesting additional attribute of this type of merit good soon becomes apparent. Often, mixing even a relatively pure market method and a pure command method is less costly than using either one alone. Thus, (a) if some kind of market is used to establish, in the first instance, a set of, say, life–convenience trade-offs, then (b) if collective decisions—even quite high-level and direct-command ones—are enacted to overrule that market and impose "more safety," (c) that assertedly more life-protective collective trade-off may not entail significant commandification costs. It may seem paradoxical, but it appears to be the case that when the government steps in and orders "more safety," people are not much troubled by the fact that such a decree is also a decision that, in fact, results in the loss of lives that a requirement of *yet more safety* would have preserved. Somehow, the collectivity has successfully placed itself on the side of life, and the costs of commandification are avoided.[21]

The result of all this is that, occasionally, our society will use one approach, relatively pure pricing, say, with respect to some of this category of merit goods, while with respect to others it will use a relatively pure command approach. But in both instances it may employ the other approach as a backup, so that its particular advantages as a decision making method can also be used. Significantly, because of the way each approach is *positioned*, the moral costs associated with its use are lessened. Indeed, much of tort law operates just this way![22]

Nevertheless, the most frequent societal reaction to the existence of this category of merit goods is to deviate both from pure market and from pure command, and to employ modified versions of each. It will sometimes use one of these singly and sometimes, in order to obtain the benefits of each that I just described, it will use the two modified approaches in concert with each other. In this respect, this category of merit goods has something in common with goods such as altruism and beneficence. These latter, which I will discuss soon enough, like merit goods of the sort I am currently talking about, also require the use of modified markets and modified command. But one should be careful. The modifications in markets and in command that effectively optimize the amount and kinds of altruism in a society are by no means necessarily the same as those modifications that best effectuate (with the lowest moral costs) the trade-offs that anti-commodification and anti-commandification merit goods require. Economic theory is asked by both categories of goods to look into and incorporate the existence and use of modified markets and modified commands. But the presence of this category of merit goods, in all likelihood, expands the scope and subtlety of the impure market and impure command approaches that economic theory must deal with, even beyond what, as we shall see in a later chapter, is needed to deal with altruism.

There is not time to go into many examples of modified approaches as responses to the requirements of this category of merit goods. A brief look at tort law and its handling of the matter will suffice, before I turn to the other—perhaps more important and, to date, less analyzed—sort of merit goods, those to which moral costs attach not because the goods are priced, but because they are allocated through the prevailing distribution of wealth.

Tort law represents a prime example of the attempted optimization and allocation—through modified markets and modified command—of merit goods that we do not wish to deal with through pure command or pure markets. Tort law does not speak of what it does as pricing lives or safety. The rubric is always that of compensating victims, of redressing wrongs, of (what is in most torts impossible) returning the victim to the *status quo* before the accident. Yet the *way* in which we do these things has the same effect as would the pricing of life and of safety. It makes those who would buy those goods—life or safety—pay the appropriate price.

Were we really only concerned with compensating worthy victims, we could compensate them in any number of ways that are far cheaper and far more effective than the means tort law uses. Similarly, were we concerned with righting wrongs, so that wrongdoers would bear burdens in accordance with their wrongdoing, we could do that much more cheaply and effectively than through torts. And if we wanted to recognize the importance of interpersonal responsibility—as some recent scholars claim is the essence of torts[23]—we could do that, perhaps using other fields of law, without the cumbersome apparatus of tort law. In fact, of course, we want to do all of the above things. It is, moreover, true that all of these goals (and others, too) are furthered by torts. It is precisely this truth that makes it "believable" that what tort law is doing is *not* pricing lives and safety, but something else, something which, just incidentally, also values those merit goods—life and safety—in the market and leads to a result that is consistent with their allocation by the market.

In effect, what we do in torts *is* to some extent pricing lives and safety, but we do this in ways that do not lead to the heavy moral costs that would be imposed if we did that pricing obviously and directly. As I'll explain in due course, doing it this way—avoiding obvious pricing—is, itself, administratively very expensive. But it is a cost we are willing to bear because the moral costs of direct pricing would be greater. This is not to say that the torts way avoids these (and other) moral costs altogether. As some distinguished scholars have pointed out,[24] what tort law does (by asserting that it seeks to compensate) is to act as if compensation can be given financially. And (in order to mimic markets) it gives more to the rich than to the poor for the same injury.[25] These attributes of tort law are, without doubt, objectionable to some.[26] They seem, however, to "cost" less morally than if we were to price safety and lives directly, or if we were to forego altogether the use of these modified markets to allocate life and safety. It is at least plausible to say that they appear to cost less because, despite these costs, we keep using such modified markets instead of any of several possible and available alternatives.[27]

But tort law does not, by any means, use only modified *markets*. Many decisions in the area reflect collective judgments and commands as well. Generally, however, these are not direct commands at the highest level. They do not manifest a "Judicial sentencing to death of a hundred young men and women." They are decentralized, often indirect in their effects, and usually positioned so that rather than seeming to allow the destruction of life and safety, they appear to put the state on the side of more life and safety preservation than individuals on the market would buy. They are, in other words, command structures that are modified in various ways. Most important, they are decentralized (particularly in their use of local courts and juries in the assessment of punitive damages, and of the prohibitory command effects these often have).[28] And they are placed so as to diminish the obviousness of the fact that they actually do permit some diminution of safety and some destruction of life. That is, they seem to demand, *collectively,* more safety, more life saving, than the market would have brought about.

There are, of course, people in society who object to tort law precisely because it employs these cumbersome mixed approaches. Thus, the pharmaceutical industry's drive for federal preemption[29] would have the effect of imposing direct, centralized, and high-level decisions as to the value of life and limb. With local tort laws preempted, it would become clear that the state at a high administrative level had decided what maximum and minimum levels of safety should apply. Who and how many would live and die would be determined transparently by centralized command. One argument *for* this is that torts costs too much.[30] On the, by no means obvious, assumption that tort law and administrative regulation are equally good—are equally effective—at setting acceptable levels of accidents,[31] this cost of tort law argument must be asserting that the moral costs of commandification are less than the economic costs (and perhaps moral costs, too) of running our torts system.[32] It is not surprising, therefore, that in some key preemption cases before the U.S. Supreme Court, the adherents of the tort law approach have emphasized how regulation led to the awful destruction of specific human lives. They have, in the context of particular cases and, of course, of particular victims, underscored the costs of commandification that preemption would impose.[33] And, just as there are proponents of more open command, so too there are those who advocate more direct and obvious pricing of life and limb. The many (painful, to me) studies seeking to ascertain and fix the proper statistical, actuarial price to be put on life and limb, and their emphasis on informing juries of these values, speak for themselves.[34]

Oh yes, both the preemption movement and the direct pricing movement have distributional consequences as well, which can also, in part, explain their supporters. And it is by no means clear whether either a pure price or a pure regulatory system would bring about "a better" *allocation* of life and limb losses (either as to amount or as to the bearers of these losses) than does torts. But this is not the place to go into all these permutations, crucially important as they are to the survival of tort law. One example of how these arguments have direct distributional significance suffices to explain why the tort debate cannot be reduced simply to the relative advantages of allocating this category of merit goods through modified markets and modified command as against purer ways.

When the pharmaceutical companies assert that the tort process is very costly, they are speaking about *costs they bear.* But if, via preemption, regulation is substituted for tort law, not only will the direct costs of regulation be different (for the moment I won't concern myself with whether they would be more or less), but the indirect costs that centralized regulation entails, the moral costs (of whatever size) of commandification that would result, would *not* be borne by the drug industry. These costs would lie on those who cannot stand having life and limb be directly assessed collectively at the highest state level. Many of the costs of tort law are today borne by the drug companies; the moral costs attendant on commandification would be borne, pretty much entirely, by people other than those companies. Who can doubt that the pharmaceutical companies have, to this extent, an important distributional reason to push for preemption and regulation, for direct commandification? This does not mean, however, that such a push is "wrong" or may not be justified for other reasons as well.[35]

It remains true, however, that our very peculiar system of torts, of mixed modified markets and commands, remains in force, and does so despite its huge costs. And there are important distributional reasons for this, too. Perhaps more people live off torts than die from them. But, even in the face of these distributional reasons behind the current system, our continued willingness to pay the very high price of tort law is striking. It seems to me to reflect, at least in part, that the moral costs of direct pricing of life and limb, like the moral costs of direct high-level regulation, may indeed also be high. To the extent that the existing torts approach avoids or reduces these, tort's own huge costs may not be as dreadful as they appear. Just as the payoffs we give to the CEOs of not-for-profit firms will, as we shall see soon enough, suggest the high value that society places on the various forms of altruism, so too our society's willingness to bear the high costs of tort law is some indication that the external *moral* costs that existing tort law helps to reduce may well be very high. And the significance of this category of merit goods is, therefore, in some sense and to some degree, confirmed.

This does not, however, mean that a proper analysis cannot come up with reform proposals that would maintain or even diminish the relatively low external moral cost of torts, while reducing significantly the system's high administrative costs. In this respect, too, the role and significance of Law and Economics scholarship is once again affirmed. And as to this as well—as to how tort law *in fact* works, as to how it and also eminent domain law mix command and pricing in the real world—specific discussion is needed. I will undertake that discussion in chapter 5 of this book.

III

Of Merit Goods and Inequality

A.

Significant as the previous category of merit goods may be, it seems to me to be nowhere near as important and widespread as the second category of such goods: the category of merit goods as to which the objection is not that it is loathsome to price them but that it is loathsome to allocate them through a prevailing wealth distribution that is highly unequal.

I think it is fair to say that as a society we are highly ambivalent with respect to wealth inequalities. On the one hand, many believe that they are needed and are inevitable if the incentives required to develop and produce the goods that the society wants are to be present and effective. And this is especially so, as will be discussed in chapter 8, if what the society deems desirable is relatively scarce. Significant wealth inequalities are, it would seem, the necessary result of our wanting a large pie filled with any number of relatively scarce fruits.

And yet many people also do not believe that existing inequalities are, in a fundamental sense, just or fair. Greater wealth, many believe, is frequently not the product of some ultimate desert but rather accrues to some because of a concatenation of not especially meritorious chance events. Whether it is the chance of the poverty or wealth into which one is born, the family and environment one is lucky or unlucky to inherit, or the mental and physical attributes one has been given—razor-sharp minds, extraordinary beauty, natural athletic prowess, on the one hand, and barely minimal skills, on the other—that have resulted in broad wealth inequality, these sources of inequality correlate only slightly, if at all, with merit. But if the attributes that we have—however unmerited—are to be converted into actions and products that are desired by society, into the common good, so to speak, then incentives to develop and use these attributes are needed. And whether the incentives are positive (financial rewards) or negative (punishment for failure to achieve), inequality results. Since in our society financial rewards are preferred to the whip by and large, the inequality that results is primarily that of wealth.[1] Little wonder, then, that attitudes toward wealth inequality are ambivalent, that in some sense we would like to have it both ways, to be equal and yet to retain incentives.[2]

This ambivalence takes many forms; my current discussion focuses on one of them. Many in our society believe that certain goods (and bads) should be made available to (or imposed on) people in ways different from the generality of goods and bads, that these goods (and bads) should be allocated in ways that do not depend primarily on the prevailing distribution of wealth. To put it in the converse, to the extent that these goods (and bads) are obtained (or avoided) as a result of wealth, many in the society are made unhappy, suffer, and object to that result. In more traditional economic language: the allocation of these goods through the prevailing wealth distribution creates significant external moral costs.

The result, not surprisingly, is that these goods (and bads) are often *not* allocated through the ordinary market. They are distributed in any number of other ways. These alternative allocative methods have occurred, I expect, in response to the desire of the bearers of such external moral costs to reduce them.[3] But, as is often the case with actions taken collectively to reduce external costs, this response has not been especially analyzed or thought out. People have simply acted. For this reason, and because these goods frequently have not been the object of systematic study, it is by no means clear that how they are handled today best combines and achieves our conflicting goals. Moreover, because some of these goods (and bads) overlap to some extent with the merit goods previously discussed— i.e., those goods the pricing of which is in itself objected to— many of the wealth distribution type of merit goods have simply been removed from the market. And this is so even though a market in them would have great advantages, were it not based on the prevailing distribution of wealth.[4]

It is time to get specific and talk about some particular goods and bads that seem to me to fall into this second— inequality objecting—category of merit goods. They are a widely diverse group of goods, and this is an important attribute because it may suggest that different treatments for different ones are appropriate. Such goods and bads run the gamut from military service (especially in wartime), through the right to have children and the right to obtain various body parts (blood, ova and semen, bone marrow, kidneys, etc.), to the right to influence elections through campaign contributions. They may also include the rights to some level of education and medical care, and possibly even to a degree of environmental protection.[5]

Virtually none of these are uncontroversially subject to (i.e., bought and sold in) the ordinary market in the United States today. Some, like military service, have been so bought and sold in the past;[6] subcategories of others, like blood, may still be;[7] yet others, like body parts generally, have been the subject of academic articles in favor of market availability;[8] and, finally, some, like campaign contributions, are the focus of heated current judicial and legislative discussion.[9] Different as these goods (and bads) are from each other, what they all have in common is that they each bring forth the same reaction in a large number of people—namely, the feeling that these are not things either that the rich should be able to get (or avoid) simply because they are rich or that the poor should be led to give up (or bear) just because of their poverty.

Not infrequently, this reaction is combined with another one, that it is wrong to price such things. In other words, the second source of merit goods is at times combined with the first, with an objection to commodification. And it is to this aspect that I would first like to turn, because I believe that, as to a significant number of these goods, the overlap is overstated.

I do not doubt that "pricing" is a problem with some of these goods. But I would suggest that, as to some, it is not a significant one and, as to others, albeit a problem, it would be substantially mitigated were the fact of pricing not also what seemingly makes the allocation of the goods dependent on the prevailing unequal distribution of wealth. To begin with the most obvious example, would a purely volunteer army, or a draft with a buyout provision as occurred in the Civil War, be objectionable, were it not for the fact that, given existing differences in wealth, these systems lead the poor to become the primary source of cannon fodder?[10] And would anyone really object to the current Supreme Court's statement that there is a First Amendment constitutional right to express oneself politically through the expenditure of one's money, were it not for the fact that such a right, if unlimited, gives the wealthy significantly greater access to political power and, in particular, allows them to buy "political goods" that in practice are not available to the poor?[11]

Let us turn to more questionable examples. Is the purchase and sale of child rights (long ago proposed by the economist Kenneth Boulding)—so that the total number of children produced would approach the socially desired level, and so that those who had children, in some fundamental sense, wanted them most—objected to based on the offensiveness of putting a price on babies, or is it primarily that it would result in the wealthy, overwhelmingly, becoming those who procreated?[12] And, perhaps most dramatically, and almost certainly with some notable differences among the goods in question, is the disgust frequently expressed at the existence of "black markets" in organs because we dislike blood, ova, and semen even being priced and especially cannot stand putting a precise money tag on kidneys, bone marrow, and livers, or is it that such markets make the rich the buyers and the poor the sellers (or, if the poor *need* an organ, the ones who die since they cannot pay the market price that the organ commands)? My own intuition is that, as to most of these goods, the principal objection has not been pricing itself but what pricing has seemed to mean, given the prevailing distribution of wealth. I would guess that, as to many of these, our attitudes would be very different were the prevailing wealth distribution substantially equal. In such a society, I would venture to say, ordinary open markets in most of the above-mentioned goods and bads would exist relatively uncontroversially.[13] And this would be so especially because, for

reasons that I will outline in a moment, market-based allocations of these goods have many great advantages.

Instead, given existing wealth differences, markets in each
of these goods are regularly objected to and frequently prohibited. The result is that these goods and bads are often allocated
by command and in ways that—when looked at carefully—are
themselves full of problems. Before I turn to those allocative
methods and their problems, however, it is useful to consider
why, despite the willingness of a seller to sell and a buyer to buy
these goods, such seemingly Paretian exchanges are often forbidden. It is often said that the prohibition is the result of pa-
ternalism, of the belief that the seller would later regret having
sold the good. And that explanation may, indeed, be true in
some instances. But there is little evidence that it is true uni-
versally. An individual who is poor may well be made better off
by selling a kidney, and may not regret it later, and yet the sale
is, nonetheless, banned.[14] Why?

Perhaps it is prohibited because many people believe that
the absence of at least a minimum of certain goods is dehuman-
izing. They feel that such goods are so fundamental that their
absence, even their willing absence, is unacceptable. We may
not permit people to sell themselves into slavery, or to forego
a minimum of education or health, simply because *we* believe
that it is immoral for people so to live, whatever they may think.
This minimum, fundamental rights explanation seems obvious
to many who are philosophically inclined.[15] It may seem problematic to those economists who find fundamental rights hard
to explain.[16] But if enough people are offended for this reason,
no other explanation for the prohibition is needed.

In any event, I can also proffer a more "utilitarian" explanation for the ban. Such sales may perhaps be prohibited because
the very presence of such sales tells the rest of us something

about how unequal our wealth distribution is, something that we are, literally, pained to hear. We do not want the inequality of wealth to be so conspicuous. But, though the sale of such goods underscores these wealth differences, it does not make us want to change the wealth differences globally because, at another level, we believe we need the incentives that have led to those differences. As a result, we feel much better if some goods are made available to those who "need" them, regardless of wealth and regardless of whether they would forego them in exchange for more wealth. The degree of wealth equality needed to keep us from feeling this way—the generalized wealth redistribution that would lead us to approve of these market exchanges—is too great. In other words, redistributing wealth generally as a way of eliminating or reducing our moral disgust at who today gets these goods and bads costs more than does their allocation in nonordinary market ways.[17]

Significantly, moreover, not all of these goods would cease to be merit ones—would stop giving rise to anguish when allocated through the prevailing market—at the same point as greater wealth equality was established. Some would no longer give rise to objections if wealth were just a little more equally distributed. Others—"fundamental rights"—would cease troubling people only were wealth distributed almost completely equally.[18]

Is all this irrational? Is it nonsense upon stilts? Economic Analysis of Law is tempted to say so. But so to call it, and to say that any removal of these goods from the ordinary market violates Pareto, is to ignore reality.[19] It fails to give weight to deeply held attitudes that have persisted in the face of that criticism. It acts as if what many feel as costs should not matter.

If, in fact, a large number of people prefer *not* to have certain goods allocated according to the prevailing wealth distribution over having changes made in the distribution that are deep enough to assuage their disgust at seeing who ends up with these goods and bads, calling that attitude irrational is less than helpful. It is, moreover, an assertion with respect to tastes and values of precisely the sort that economists assert they are not permitted to make. As a result, regardless of whether my possible explanations for the anguish felt are correct, or if that disgust arises for any other reason, the economist *cannot* deny its presence and ignore its effects. Taking individuals' utilities as they are means that such prohibitions are *not* Pareto inferior.[20] It is far better, then, to accept the existence of such wealth distribution–dependent merit goods and to examine which ways of allocating them avoid or mitigate both the moral costs of their allocation through the ordinary market and the costs of dramatic generalized wealth redistributions.[21]

B.

The most obvious way of dealing with such goods (and the most common) is to remove them from the market and to allocate them collectively by command. This approach, however, has two fundamental problems, each of which deserves attention. The first is that different people desire these goods and bads differently. If, in other words, they were allocated in a market that derived from a totally equal wealth distribution, some people would bid for a great deal of some of these and forego others, while other people would seek to accrue a totally different combination. That means that an equal distribution of these goods and bads would be anything but a good one.

The second fundamental problem derives from the first. It is that any collective allocation of these goods that is not "the same to each and all" will be greatly influenced by the prevailing distribution of power. Even assuming that a collective allocation did as good a job as do markets at teasing out the relative desire of different people for different goods, including these merit goods, it would remain the case that the allocation—and the analysis of relative wants and needs—would be significantly dependent on, and biased by, who has more power and who has less. The moral costs that arose from the market allocation of these goods and bads derived from the market's dependence on a highly unequal distribution of wealth. But analogous, and potentially as great or greater, moral costs might well attach to the allocation of these goods collectively, since that allocation would be dependent on the distribution of power.[22] And that distribution is no more acceptable, and no more changeable without huge costs, than is the distribution of wealth. The history of the collective allocation of some of these goods in the past, outlined in *Tragic Choices,* shows how quickly external moral costs of command allocation can become unacceptably great.[23]

What, then, are we to do? We can try to set up modified collective allocation schemes that seek to discern different people's desires for these different goods and bads, and that involve a less dramatically unequal distribution of power than prevails generally. Or we can seek to modify markets, so that the market methods that are used with respect to these goods do not depend on the generally prevailing distribution of wealth. Each is worth some further discussion.

The first possible approach—modified command structures—was examined more generally, and without a specific focus on merit goods, in *Tragic Choices.* And the advantages and problems that adhere to those modifications were there canvassed. A couple of things, however, remain worth saying. First, as I will say apropos of altruism, if economics is to be used to gauge legal structures, it is essential for it to consider our common use of complex and often private command structures and not to focus (even just psychologically) on command as a simple, single, centralized governmental method. Again, as I shall discuss later in more detail,[24] the fact that the command structure noted by Coase in "The Nature of the Firm" involved decentralized private command relationships is worth underscoring.[25]

Second, a few of the advantages of modified command structures in dealing with this category of merit goods should be noted. The most obvious is that such modified command decisions can be made subject to a different distribution of power than prevails "overall." Local power, for example, is also distributed unequally, but its unequal distribution frequently differs from that of centralized power. The questions then become: As to each of these merit goods, what level of local, regional, or national command decision reflects a distribution of power that causes the lowest external moral costs? What power advantages and differences do people object to least as to each of these goods—which, in some idealized sense, people would like to have distributed "equally," where equally means not the same amount to each but rather an allocation that results from an adequately power-equal decision making structure? And can such a structure, in fact, be set up to handle that particular merit good?

Tragic Choices noted the use of localized draft boards to administer broadly worded selective service laws and to decide who should be drafted and who should be deferred.[26] And it is worth underscoring that personal attributes and influence play very differently at a local level than they do nationally. My own experience during the Korean War reflected that. It was clear to me that my extended deferment was due in significant part (and with no attempt, by me, to rely on that) to the fact that I am an Italian American because, in New Haven, Connecticut, in 1952, that ethnicity had a local political significance that it did not have nationally or probably even in Connecticut as a whole.[27]

A second advantage is that modified, and often local, command structures may be better able than centralized ones to take into account different relative desires for the good and abhorrence of the bad among possible recipients. Modified command structures may succeed in doing tolerably well what markets seek to do and what centralized command has difficulty doing—namely, discerning different desires and needs among different individuals as to any particular merit good. Again, the point is discussed in *Tragic Choices*. And, again, the capacity of the modified decision making structure to discern the difference in desire will vary with respect to different particular merit goods. Moreover, the importance of responding to that difference—the degree to which an *equal* allocation ("bananas equally to all") is undesirable because desires differ—varies with different merit goods. This possible variance is why, if merit goods of this sort are to be allocated through modified command structures, it by no means follows that a legal system will use the same structures for all of them. Not only will the modified command structures vary; the decision as to whether modified command or modified markets will be used may also differ with respect to different merit goods.

The question, however, remains the same. If pure markets that depend on our generalized wealth distribution and pure command that depends on overall general power distribution cause large external moral costs when applied to the allocation of certain goods, what modifications—whether of market or of command structures—reduce those external moral costs most for each good in that category, while at the same time giving recognition to actual differences in people's desire for that particular good? This question, by no means easy in itself, is rendered still more complex by the fact that any modified command and modified market structures can get overwhelmed. A structure that may handle the allocation of one or two of these goods pretty well may become quite inadequate if asked to allocate all of them. That means that the above question must be modified to ask which of these modified structures have a comparative advantage in the allocation of which particular goods. The ultimate choice of structures that a legal system makes must reflect this inability to do more than *some* things well. It must, in effect, do a very complex job of joint maximization. And this choice among structures, not so incidentally, is once again a reason why law *does* need economics!

Was the decision by Local Board 10 to defer Guido Calabresi in 1952 so that he could go to Oxford to study economics a good one? Was it a fair one? I have my views on both of these, of course. For the present, however, what needs to be said is that a structure was put in place that (a) did not allocate military service in the Korean War through the market (pure or modified); (b) reflected local influence and power more than national power; (c) was capable, to some degree, of discerning differences in desire and reluctance of different individuals to serve; and (d) evaluated—based on local influences and values—the relation of that desire and reluctance to some perception of collective needs. Whether that structure reduced external moral costs significantly is hard to say. The moral disgust at pure market allocations, the poor as cannon fodder, was avoided. But it may well be that another external cost, one that was just as great, was created. The Korean War draft system did give rise to the perception that the smart, the college kids, the friends of local politicians avoided the bad. I do not know how great *those* costs were. At the time, however, they seemed preferable to the moral costs associated with a pure market. Whether they were higher or lower than the costs that would have flowed from a *modified* market is hard to say because, at the time, no such structure was adequately proposed either by lawyers or economists.

C.

What would such modified market structures look like and when might they be used? Let me list three possibilities, each of which is also talked about more generally in *Tragic Choices:* (a) a system akin to rationing as used in World War II; (b) a tax-or subsidy-structured, (relatively) wealth distribution– neutral market; and (c) a market in which the medium of exchange is not money but some other widely held good, such as time.[28] Each of these offers a possible means of reducing the external moral costs that result from allocations of this category of merit goods through an unfettered market, and each seeks—while delinking desire from the general wealth distribution—to ascertain individuals' relative desire for the good (or abhorrence of the bad) with respect to a particular merit good. As such, and as with modified command structures, the potential desirability of each modification discussed may well differ with respect to the different specific merit goods to be allocated.

The first example of a modified market approach that I will consider is analogous to, and derives from, a couple of rationing systems employed in the United States in World War II. During that war, allocation of many goods through the ordinary market was, for a variety of reasons, deemed undesirable. Some of these reasons were analogous to those that define the category of merit goods here under discussion. Others were related to the fact that (for yet other reasons) price controls were considered necessary in wartime with the result that the ordinary market would not be able to allocate these goods. The kind of "bidding" that normally decides who gets what goods and how much of each good gets produced had to be cut off since it was inconsistent with controlled prices. It was not so much that bidding would mean that the rich would get more of these goods—the usual effect of ordinary markets—as that ordinary market bidding could not be permitted at all. This is not to say that the inequality reasons that adhere to the merit good categories under discussion were not at play as well. Indeed, it seems clear that the external moral costs that usually attach to only a few special goods and bads became, in total war, significant for goods that the free market allocates in peacetime without giving rise to significant pains or regrets. In total war, it was commonplace to feel that all should be equal. Moreover, it was widely believed that during such a war, and for a limited time, the financial incentives that are the source of wealth inequality could and should be put aside and replaced by direct command.[29]

In any event, once ordinary bidding was prohibited, another way of sorting out who got which goods in relation to individuals' relative desire for them had to be established. And it had to be established for a wide variety of ordinary goods, not just for those that today would be viewed as merit goods. That system was rationing, and its structure helps us understand one way in which markets can be modified to deal with merit goods.

A few goods were assigned directly by command. Not everyone got the same amount, but the decisions as to who should get how much was a collective one, made and applied

at different levels of government on the basis of collective judgments as to collective utility and (perhaps) appropriate individual desire. Gasoline was so assigned, and my father, as a
doctor, got relatively much. Others got significantly less.
Frankly, I do not remember whether these others could ask for
more on the basis of special "needs" (and whether such needs,
in fact, represented, to some extent, special desires). For present
purposes it does not matter because one could have a system
that worked either way. What *is* significant is that trades were
not permitted. My dad was not allowed to exchange any excess
gasoline with someone else for goods that my father might have
wanted more. Gasoline rationing was, in this crucial sense, a
modified collective approach to allocation rather than a modified market approach.

Other forms of rationing constituted instead paradigmatic modified markets. A great variety of goods were rationed
according to a system of color-coded stamps. A relatively small
number of goods deemed to be in particularly short supply—
butter, meats, fats, etc.—were in the red category. Each good in
this category carried a *price* in red stamps. That meant that one
could get more, even much more, of some of these goods, if
one was willing to forego (or limit the amount obtained of)
other red-stamp goods. In other words, people could express
their relative desire for the goods in this category by their
response to the red-stamp price of each.

In effect, they could trade with each other on the basis of
relative desire—and do so without actually exchanging goods—
precisely as occurs in the ordinary market. The difference between the red-stamp market and the ordinary one was, first,
that the red-stamp prices were *collectively* set so that the market
would clear—more needs to be said later about this aspect of
the system. Second, and most crucially for present purposes,

the distribution on the basis of which those relative desires were expressed was *not* the ordinary distribution of wealth but rather the number of red stamps assigned to each household. In theory, red stamps could be given "equally" to all, or they might, instead, be assigned "unequally," with some households getting more than others, presumably on the basis of some collectively determined notions of fairness. The point is that, either way, a degree of responsiveness to individual desires was not merely permitted but positively recognized, and the distribution of red-stamp "wealth" (on the basis of which these differences in desire manifested themselves) reflected collective decisions designed in part, I would assert, to reduce the external moral costs that flowed from the resulting allocation of red-stamp goods.

Green stamps worked much the same way but encompassed a far broader number of goods. And there were no trade-offs between red- and green-stamp goods. The result was that—whereas a great desire for a large quantity of red-stamp goods might go unfulfilled because one simply could not give up enough other red-stamp goods to get that much of one, given the number of red stamps made available and the price of each red-stamp good—within the green-stamp category, and subject to the distribution of green stamps, one could get pretty much as large an amount of the good as one wanted. In other words, in classic economic terms, one could obtain as much of a desired green-stamp good as one was willing to forego in other such goods. Again, the distribution of green stamps was collectively determined, as were the prices that allowed the market in green stamps to clear. But, within these limits, the green-stamp market operated very much like an ordinary market: individuals expressed their desires for a broad expanse of goods based on the distribution of green-stamp "wealth."

But what is one to say of the fact that (a) the number and distribution of green and red stamps across the society, (b) what goods were subject to each, without trade-offs across red and green, and (c) the price of each good in stamps were all collectively determined? In the ordinary market, how much is produced in total and, hence, also the prices that "clear" the market in those goods are themselves decided by the market. Under rationing, such decisions were made differently. And I need to discuss (a) the reason for and consequences of this fact for merit goods as well as (b) the significance of the decision *not* to ration some goods at all, even in wartime—i.e., *not* to subject some goods to green or red stamps or, like gasoline, to direct allocation methods—but instead to permit ordinary markets to determine both the total amount produced and the prices of these unrationed goods.

The fact that only some goods were made subject to wartime rationing, and that different approaches were used with respect to different goods that were rationed, is instructive of what can be done in ordinary times with different merit goods. In a real sense, what wartime rationing meant was that many goods that in ordinary times would not be viewed as merit goods were in wartime so considered. That not all goods were so treated told us that, even in wartime, ordinary markets were preferred for allocating a wide variety of goods: those that were not rationed. In other words, the external (in part moral) costs that were deemed too significant to ignore in wartime still did not attach to all goods, although they attached to many more goods than to those relatively few we consider merit ones in peacetime. A collective decision had to be made as to which goods could be allocated through ordinary (i.e., wealth distribution–dependent) markets in the circumstances of World War II and which should, instead, be allocated in ways that removed the influence of wealth differences from their allocation.

That same decision needs to be made—indeed, if one but looks, one sees *is* made—as to merit goods in peacetime. The number of goods removed from the ordinary market is much smaller in peacetime, and the type of goods so removed is of a sort that is different from those treated that way in wartime. But the collective decision is of the same sort: How do we best reduce the external moral costs (and especially in wartime, perhaps other external costs as well) of ordinary market allocations, while retaining the desirable incentives that reliance on markets creates? How many goods, and which ones, should be removed from the ordinary market and made subject to a modified market allocation (or to a nonmarket allocation) so as to accomplish this optimally? The fact that many market incentives are temporarily attenuated in wartime, and that the costs of ordinary markets in wartime are far greater and adhere to many more goods than in peacetime, explains the difference between the wartime and peacetime outcomes of that collective decision. It determines which and how many goods are removed from the ordinary market. It changes, however, neither the nature of the decision nor the fact that such a decision *is* made.

Of similar significance for the analysis of merit goods is the fact that not all goods that were removed from the ordinary market were made subject to the same allocation scheme in World War II. Some goods—those subject to green stamps— were allocated in a way that mimicked the market in the breadth of concern that the scheme showed for the preservation of in-dividual choices; green-stamp allocation enabled individuals to show very significantly and effectively their preferences for some goods by foregoing alternative goods. Other goods—those subject to red stamps—were allocated in a way that allowed preferences to be shown in terms of alternatives foregone but only to a much more limited extent. Finally, still other goods, like gasoline, were allocated in ways that showed no concern with individual desire as expressed in a modified market. As to these last goods, to the extent that differences in desire were allowed to influence the allocation at all, it was through pressure on the collective decision makers and not through individual trade-offs, that is, not through individual decisions to forego alternative goods.

The same choices can be made—and I would suggest *are* made—with respect to those goods that are deemed merit ones in peacetime. Here, as with the wartime decision, the choice of how to treat which goods depends on (a) which allocative approaches reduce the external moral costs (including the costs not only of wealth dependence but also of commodification and commandification—on which I will have more to say later); (b) the extent of differences in desire for (or abhorrence of) specific merit goods among different people and the confidence that we place in a system based on the foregoing of alternatives as a way of elucidating those differences in desire; and (c) collective desiderata as to who should get the goods and bads—that is, collective preferences with respect to allocation that exist *apart from* individual preferences, however well the latter might be expressed by individuals' foregoing of alternative goods. Since these differ widely with different merit goods, it should not be surprising that not all merit goods are treated the same way.

But it does not follow that the way we today treat such merit goods is optimal. Recognition of the existence of such goods, and careful analysis of which goods are deemed merit ones and of why they are so viewed, could lead to the development of economic models that permit us, instead of treating such goods as aberrations, to say why, and in what circumstances, some approaches to these goods are better than others.

This analysis may well lead us to criticize and reform existing approaches and to urge the adoption of other approaches. If we start from an analysis of actually existing treatments of merit goods and derive from that analysis models to explain the benefits and costs of alternative treatments of such goods, then these more nuanced models obtained as a result of what I call Law and Economics can do what traditional Economic Analysis of Law does so powerfully—namely, they can help us to confirm, abandon, or reform current treatments of merit goods.

D.

I need to return, however, to an important way in which rationing differs from the ordinary market, in addition to removing the resulting allocation from dependence on the prevailing wealth distribution. Even in a green-stamp rationing system, which is highly sensitive to market values, the total amounts of each good produced and the prices that clear the market are not market-determined but collectively set. Of course, the command decision as to how many fruits and vegetables will be produced in wartime may be collectively determined by reference to what is happening in the green-stamp market. And the same is true of the prices in green stamps that the collectivity assigns to different green-stamp goods. The government decision makers will undoubtedly be affected by what the responses of individuals in the green-stamp market disclose about relative desire for alternate goods. But such collective decisions, both as to how much of each green-stamp good to make available and as to the price set on it to clear the market, are not market decisions. By way of contrast, in ordinary markets, atomistic decisions affect both the total produced and the prices that attach to different products.

To use the terminology that Philip Bobbitt and I used in *Tragic Choices,* in green-stamp markets, the first-order decisions as to how much of each good or bad is to be made available for allocation and as to the resulting green-stamp prices that will clear that market are collectively made.[30] In wartime this modified command structure was both desired and considered desirable. The resources assigned to the making of green- and red-stamp goods were deemed proper matters for centralized decisions. But the same is by no means true for all or most merit goods in peacetime. Of course, as to some such goods, the first-order decision will almost invariably be viewed as best made collectively. How many are needed to serve in the military may well be one such decision.[31] But, as to other merit goods, that is often not the case. That we may want to allow people to buy and sell organs (but *only* if that market does not depend on the prevailing wealth distribution) does not mean that we believe that the total number of organs—live and dead—made available is best decided collectively rather than as a result of individual responses in a market. Unlike perhaps as to military service, in the case of organs, if a wealth distribution–neutral market could be established, individual responses in that market might desirably determine the quantity and type of organs actually proffered for transplant. As to organs, the first-order decision is not necessarily best made collectively.

But is it possible to establish a modified market that removes (or attenuates) the influence of the prevailing wealth distribution from the expression of preferences yet still allows individuals to determine the total availability of the good and bad, making the first-order decision atomistically? The rationing approach cannot accomplish both at once. But another form of modified market that I mentioned earlier may be able to do so. Such a modified market may be achieved by attenuating or eliminating the effects of prevailing wealth differences through taxes and subsidies.

Before I turn to what such a modified market might look like, however, I would like, once again, to emphasize that the desirability and feasibility of having the first-order decision made either collectively or through the market will likely vary with different merit goods. Accordingly, just as the use of modified command as against modified markets will differ as to different merit goods, so too will the use of different types of market modifications. For some merit goods, as I hope to show in due course, a green-stamp or even a red-stamp rationing system will work very well. For others, a tax/subsidy approach will seem more desirable.

The structure of a wealth distribution–neutral market effectuated through taxes and subsidies is easily described. I will outline such a market in its purest and most extreme form, one in which choices are as independent of prevailing wealth differences as they would be in a green-stamp rationing system in which everyone got an equal number of green stamps. But just as a rationing system can create its own unequal "green-stamp wealth" or mimic, but attenuate, the prevailing wealth distribution, so too can a tax- or subsidy-modified market. In other words, such a market can simply reduce (but not do away with) the influence of the prevailing wealth distribution, or it can create an unequal wealth distribution that is specifically desired for purposes of the allocation of that particular merit good. Which is done will depend on what is thought to reduce the external moral costs that adhere to that good, and on how costly, in a fairly ordinary sense, the establishment and administration of a particular tax/subsidy scheme is with respect to that specific good.

Suppose we want people to express their desire to serve or to avoid service in the military in monetary terms but do not wish to make that expression derive from the amount of wealth people have. Suppose, in other words, that we want to gauge what people's desire would be if the distribution of wealth were equal.[32] How would we do it through taxes and subsidies? There are various ways. We could, for instance, draft everyone in the appropriate category (by age, etc.) and then, mimicking but modifying the Civil War system, let each individual buy his or her way out, making the buyout price differ, however, with a person's wealth. For the highest wealth category, the cost of purchasing a so-called substitute (the Civil War term) would be extremely high; for the poorest, very low. One could set these prices so that the same percentage of people from each wealth category ended up serving. Alternatively, one could have a purely volunteer army instead of a draft, but a volunteer army in which the payment to serve differed according to wealth. Under this structure, the richest would be paid greatly to serve, the poorest not much. But, once again, the "prices" (i.e., payment for volunteering) could be set so that an equivalent percentage of volunteers would come from each wealth bracket. The money needed to fund such a system could be raised by taxation of whatever degree of progressivity one wished. Finally, one could do a mixture of the two. In effect, one could tax the richest a large amount for nonservice, while simply paying the poor to serve. Here, too, the taxes and payments could be set to achieve an equal percentage of conscripts and volunteers from each wealth category.

There are obvious problems with each of these (and any other yet more mixed schemes). As noted in *Tragic Choices*, an equal percentage from each wealth category would not accurately gauge desire to serve or to avoid service cleansed of wealth differences if, as is not unlikely, attitude toward service correlated with wealth differences for reasons not dependent on wealth. (If people of a particularly militaristic or pacifistic ethnic or cultural tradition were, in the relevant country, disproportionately found in one or another wealth bracket.) And what would be appropriate wealth brackets anyway? (How does one treat the debt-ridden graduate of a great law school who has immense wealth-making potential in comparison to a debt-free, decent-earning artisan of the same age who is already at his or her earning peak?)[33]

More important, would we want perfect wealth neutrality even if we could get it? If the object is to assign a merit good or bad so that the moral costs that adhere when the allocation is based on the prevailing wealth distribution are reduced, but to do so without incurring too large "ordinary" costs in order to attenuate these "moral" costs, it is by no means clear that perfect wealth neutrality (even if we could get it) would be what is sought. Moreover, just as society might want to allocate green stamps unequally (if in a different way or to a different degree from the prevailing distribution of wealth), so too a society might wish the allocation of the particular merit good (here, selective service) to respond to unequal distribution–based incentives.

But all that, in the end, is beside the point that I am trying to make. In seeking to separate market incentives from the prevailing wealth distribution, we need not make the perfect be the enemy of the good. Seeming "perfection," even if desirable and feasible, may cost too much, and a far less radical tax/subsidy scheme might well go a long way toward reducing the moral costs that adhere to a full Civil War scheme (i.e., a wealth-dependent selective service market), whether of the purely volunteer or purely buyout varieties. A far less extreme set of higher prices than those posited above might nonetheless mean that a good many rich as well as poor served, and that result might well be all that is wanted or needed. To the extent that equality of incentives to serve is *not* desired as to different wealth categories, the tax/subsidy scheme imposed could reflect that dimension of desire as readily as could a green-stamp system in which the stamps were assigned unequally.

My point is not to suggest what scheme is best for any merit good in any society. My aim rather is twofold: (a) to show, first, that tax/subsidy schemes are available, as alternatives to a rationing approach, for assessing relative desire independently of the prevailing wealth distributions; and (b) to demonstrate that such schemes have some advantages over rationing approaches when dealing with peacetime merit goods.

The first of these advantages is that a modified market-type rationing scheme requires there to be included in the scheme a significant number of goods that are tradable. Since market-mimicking rationing gauges desire in terms of direct alternatives foregone, those alternatives must also be rationed to be made part of the scheme. Only if a largish number of other "green" goods are included can we test relative individual desire for, say, broccoli, which—let us assume—was the good that we wanted to remove from the ordinary market. In wartime rationing this was not a problem because we wanted many goods to be removed from the ordinary market, and hence a broad set of alternatives to choose among arose easily. In peacetime that is rarely the case.

In peacetime, we may not want to remove a similarly large set of diverse goods of like kind from the ordinary market. To set up a rationing scheme, then, we would need to include in the pool of tradable goods many goods that we do not consider to be merit ones. And the inclusion of nonmerit goods is obviously costly, both in itself and in terms of the effect that it could have on the incentives to which the ordinary wealth distribution relates. It is especially a problem because simply setting up a rationing pool that includes all the different goods to which our society gives merit status in peacetime will not do. For the tradable pool to work, the goods in the pool have to be viewed by individuals as substitutable for each other to a significant extent, that is, as *alternatives* to forego. Putting body parts, child rights, military service, and political contributions in one pool and letting people choose among them, and *only among them*, may do great harm to individual desires and, in that sense, may be more costly than is justified by the scheme's other benefits.[34]

Tax/subsidy schemes of all sorts avoid this problem. They do so because they operate in terms of money. Unlike rationing schemes, tax/subsidy schemes do not restrict the alternatives that can be foregone to a limited group. Instead, like the ordinary market, they gauge desire in terms of the willingness to forego the universality of goods that are subject to the market. What is adequately substitutable becomes a matter of individual preference. What tax/subsidy schemes do is affect the price of the merit good in question, so that demand for it is distanced from general wealth. Apart from that, however, such schemes leave unaltered the range of alternatives that one can forego.

The second potential advantage of tax/subsidy schemes over rationing ones is that they do not necessarily require the collectivity (a) to make the first-order decisions and (b) to set prices that will clear the market in accordance with that decision. The polity does not *need* to decide collectively how much of the merit good or bad is desired in society. In the example I just used—selective service—we normally assume that the first-order decision *is* made collectively. How many soldiers are wanted, needed, is not normally believed to be best left to individual market choices.[35] But that is not necessarily the case with other merit goods. A society might well wish to have the allocation of body parts made in a way that is totally or partially distanced from the prevailing wealth distributions,[36] and yet wish to leave to the market—to an aggregate of individual decisions—the total number of kidneys, bone marrows, blood, etc., that are available, as well as whether that availability is from live or dead donors.[37]

If the merit good in question is the right to have children, a society might very well determine collectively the total population size that it desires and, hence, the number of children that it wishes to be born. And if the society does make such a collective determination, it can—through rationing or tax/subsidy schemes—allocate child rights in relatively wealth-neutral ways. But the society might also be agnostic on the total population question and still not wish the number of children born to belong disproportionately to parents in certain wealth brackets. If that is the case, it could use a tax/subsidy scheme to "equalize" who has children, by charging different relative amounts for child rights, yet do so in a way that leaves open the total number of children that will result.

E.

None of what I have said so far implies that rationing schemes may not be preferable to tax/subsidy schemes as to some merit goods even in peacetime. Consider the selective service example again. Here, the first-order decision as to the total number of people wanted in the army may well be best made collectively.[38] Hence, the potential advantage of tax/subsidy schemes in not requiring collectivity would not apply. Moreover, as to this merit good, there might also be a readily available set of tradable alternatives that the society does not mind removing (or perhaps even wishes to remove) from the ordinary market and making part of, so to speak, a "green-stamp pool." If that society believes that collective service for a certain number of years is desirable for its youths, and that fulfilling this obligation in one way or another should not be voluntary, then a group of reasonable substitutes for military service would be readily at hand. For this to be the case, non-military service need not be viewed as a merit good, in the sense that I have defined such goods. All that is needed is that the society collectively want to make youth service obligatory (as it does education).[39] The reasons for that collective decision are immaterial here. What matters is only that such service is compulsory and that its forms represent foregoable alternatives that are adequate substitutes to the merit good in question: military service.

If these two conditions are met, a rationing scheme could easily be set up (and indeed has even from time to time been suggested as desirable, quite apart from any formal analysis). Youths, say, would be required to serve a certain term, but whether in the military—including whether in the army, navy, air force, or marines, at home or abroad, in war zones or not— or outside the military altogether would, in a sense, be up to them. Alternatives could include service in an international peace corps (in different types of countries), domestic equivalents (whether teaching or involving physical labor, in varied American "needy" zones). They might, if so desired, even include some forms of education to be followed by use of that education in underserved areas (e.g., medical primary care in places where few doctors now practice).

Once the number and types and subtypes (service in one country or another) of alternatives to be made available were settled on, each subject individual would be free to choose where and how to spend his or her time. The length of service in each category and subcategory would be set so as to meet the collectively determined need for military bodies of various sorts (the required cannon fodder, so to speak). Their prices would be set to satisfy the collectively determined need for the merit bad that we have been talking about. But they would also be set to clear the market in all the other forms and subforms of service that were included in the scheme. Just as the green-stamp price of broccoli and of breakfast cereals was set to reflect relative desire for each in relation to the total amount of the good made available, so too service in, say, sunny Italy or rainy England would be priced to take into account how much each was favored or disfavored by those who had to choose. A pure rationing allocation scheme would be established. Indeed, if one wanted—unnecessarily—to make the analogy more direct, a green-stamp book could be given to each subject individual, with the requirement that the green stamps had to be worked off, and the price set for the removal of the stamps from the book would vary with the different forms of service being allocated. Finally, in such a scheme there would be no need to impose the requirement of service equally on everyone. Just as green stamps did not have to be distributed equally, so too, if the society desired, some individuals could be exempted from service, either fully or in part.[40] The governing distribution, though different from the prevailing wealth distribution, would reflect whatever differences the society wanted to recognize.

How many of the goods and bads we currently deem to be merit ones could be made subject to rationing? Might one, for instance, set up a pool that could work and include all manner of body parts in exchange for the guaranteed right to get body parts, as needed, in the future? Would one want to include in that pool child rights, which, like body parts, involve life values, albeit perhaps of a very different sort? And what would be the advantages and disadvantages of dealing with these merit goods in this way, rather than by a tax/subsidy scheme or more directly, collectively? None of these are for me to say, and certainly not in this essay. My object here is just to point out what we can do—and what we, in fact, already do—to remove some goods from the prevailing wealth distribution or to attenuate the influence of this distribution on the allocation of such goods. The analysis of how best to do that, as to what goods in which societies, is exactly the work that I hope sophisticated lawyer-economists will undertake.

F.

One additional way of reducing the importance of the prevailing distribution of wealth on the allocation of merit goods needs to be mentioned. That is to make the allocation of such goods subject to a medium of exchange that is already broadly in being—for example, time. This approach differs from rationing in that we need not create the medium of exchange (as with green stamps); it is already there. Nor do we need to create the pool of tradable goods. Time is already used to allocate or influence the allocation of many goods in our society. Time, moreover, can be used to allocate goods in ways that would in practice differ both from ordinary market and ordinary command allocations. But the prevailing distribution of time, like the distribution of power and wealth, is by no means equal. Just as power and wealth are unequally distributed, and their unequal distributions differ to some extent from each other, so too is time unequally distributed, and its distribution differs from that of both wealth and power. (Other generally available non-wealth-based and non-power-based means of allocation will likely have analogous features.)

Significantly, time is also exchangeable for money and power, but only in complex and somewhat indirect ways. I can pay someone to stand in line for me. Or, if I have the authority, I can use some of my authority to order a person to stand in line for me. But there are things which only I can or am allowed to do, and that are assessed only in terms of time. The relationship is complicated. I cannot pay someone else to go through customs for me at the border. Yet, if I am a diplomat, I can go through a special line and save time. And I may, for a price, be able to get on a specially preexamined entry list that diminishes waiting greatly. Moreover, a society can assess differently the amounts of time needed by different individuals to get particular goods. It can do so based on its judgments as to the inequality of the underlying distribution of time or the particular value of time to that person. Thus, not only a diplomat but also an elderly or sick person may get the benefit of a different, speedier customs line.

All this is made much more complex by the fact that the determination of the underlying distribution of time is anything but easy. The issue is not just the amount of time one has but also what the time one has is worth, in terms of available alternatives that one foregoes through the use of one's time. An old person has less time left than a young one. But to the extent that the old person has fewer things available to him or her on which to spend time (because that person, say, is no longer working and cannot, for health reasons, engage in many forms of play), his or her limited time may, in fact, be distributionally quite large relative to the much greater time seemingly available to a younger person, whose time is, however, subject to a large number of demands.

Nevertheless, means of allocation like time—which, like wealth and power, are generally available but are both different and differently distributed than wealth and power—can be, and to some extent are, used to allocate merit goods. Indeed, in my selective service example, time was employed directly as the equivalent of a green-stamp price to effectuate the exchanges among the items in the rationing pool. Even a preliminary discussion, let alone a full one, of how such alternative mediums of exchange can be used is well beyond the scope of this essay. The principal reason for mentioning these alternatives—time in particular—is to underscore that (a) all mediums of exchange (including wealth and power) that are already in existence and not artificially created (like green stamps) are, to varying degrees, distributed unequally; (b) these inequalities differ from each other, and may to some extent attenuate each other, but may also, at times, exacerbate each other (e.g., wealth and power may be highly correlated); and (c) to the extent that exchanges among these alternatives are not prohibited (and such prohibitions are usually very costly),[41] individuals will use the medium of which they have much to obtain more of that of which they have less, thereby getting the goods that are primarily allocated through that "obtained" medium. (Not only will people pay others to stand in line for them; they will also make political contributions and perhaps even bribe in order to buy, in a sense, what power rather than money allocates.) Hence, any discussion of optimal ways of allocating the goods and bads that society deems to be merit ones requires truly careful study, modeling, and analysis. But since we, in fact, do allocate such goods in nonordinary market ways, and do it all the time, studies that help us say whether we are doing it well—in view of the costs of alternative approaches—are, I would argue, more than worth undertaking. They are essential! Nevertheless, they are beyond the scope of this book.

IV
Of Merit Goods Generally
Specific Applications and Concluding Thoughts

A.

What, then, are we to say here about merit goods, (a) as to what they are; (b) how they might best be handled; and (c) why a society might well wish to handle them in these ways rather than by altering its general wealth distribution?[1] Let us consider some that I have suggested fit the category and others that might or might not fit.

Among the goods and bads that I have implicitly and occasionally explicitly been placing in this group of merit goods that people are averse to conditioning on wealth distribution are military service, transplantable body parts, child rights, and campaign contributions. Others—whose treatment, in our and in cognate societies, indicates that they might fit in the category—are a basic level of education, of health care, and of environmental protection. As to almost all of these it seems likely that a wide group of people, if asked, would say something like, "It would be wrong to have these allocated so that the rich get them and the poor don't." Why many people seem to feel that way, and with particular intensity, about these goods and not so much about others—as I have said—is beside the point. To ask whether such attitudes are "right," "make sense"—or, as is sometimes done, "are consistent with Pareto optimality"[2]—is to engage in precisely the kind of taste/value assertions that economics says it eschews. It is, as I will more fully discuss in later essays (which will also speak to what, instead, economics *can and should* tell us about tastes and values), as misguided as it would be to ask why some people like caviar and others bananas.

If a sufficient number of people "object to" the allocation of these goods and bads according to the prevailing wealth distribution and "suffer" if they are so allocated, then the cost of that suffering must be taken into account, just as the desire for, or the abhorrence of, any other—more traditional—good or bad by many people cannot be ignored. The fact that there are different ways of diminishing these wealth distribution–dependent moral costs, with lesser or greater costs of their own, is certainly worth examining. But the existence of these costs must, in one sense, be taken by economists to be as much a given as are the costs of producing an optimal amount of traditional goods. It is a given, moreover, that explains many of the actual legal structures we see around us. And it is a given which, if treated as such, helps one to criticize, reform, or confirm the desirability of the particular legal structures used. Just as it is worthwhile to try to find ways of producing wheat more efficiently, so it is worthwhile to search for less "costly" ways of allocating merit goods!

But is it not also the case that if one were to ask many people about virtually *any* good, they would say that it would be better if that good were allocated in a way that depended less than is actually the case on the existing distribution of wealth? And yet, most such goods and bads continue to be allocated on the basis of the prevailing wealth distribution. Why is that? The reason is important if we are to understand how merit goods are, and ought to be, handled. It lies in the earlier-mentioned ambivalence that many people feel toward equality, an ambivalence that manifests itself in many of our legal structures. On the one hand, many people prefer equality to inequality.[3] On the other hand, many of these same people believe that a considerable amount of inequality is inevitable if we are to have the kinds of incentives needed to make more available for all to share (however unequally).[4]

It is this ambivalence that explains the seeming paradox described above. If only the specific good about whose allocation people were being asked was involved, then making it available "equally"[5] would further the respondents' desire for greater equality. And, because only that good was being removed from ordinary market allocation, the negative effect on incentives would be minimal. The gain in equality—*pleasure*—would outweigh any loss of incentive—*cost!* Hence, the answer.[6] But, since the good being asked about is little different from the vast majority of goods, removing it from the market, as a practical matter, would logically entail removing a lot of other goods from the market as well. And the result of that would be an unacceptable diminution of incentives. Thus, in practice, the good which, if singled out, would desirably be allocated in a way that is more egalitarian than occurs through the ordinary market ends up being allocated by that market, and not in derogation of it.

How then does a society choose which goods to remove from the market? How does it decide which to treat as merit goods? The choice, in practice, is the result of a kind of comparative advantage decision. Which goods, if removed from ordinary markets, reduce the external moral costs of inegalitarianism most, with the least negative effect on incentives? That is the question societies ask themselves, whether implicitly or explicitly. And the answer to that question can be seen in the nonordinary market treatment of only some selected goods. The question, it should be understood, is a double one. Those very goods whose ordinary market allocation causes the most external moral costs are also the goods whose market allocation, because of their importance, may create the greatest incentives. Society in practice asks itself what is lost and what is gained as to each possible allocation. And this, incidentally, may well explain the mixed treatment of some of these goods, like education and health care. A minimum amount of each is removed from the ordinary market and made available in some relatively egalitarian way. But above that minimum, the ordinary market rules, and does so with a vengeance. It is not hard to see, in this common societal legal structure, a reflection of the competing costs and benefits.

But if the existing legal structures suggest a series of decisions as to which goods and bads, if removed to a lesser or greater extent from the market, gain that particular society the most in reduction of inequality costs in relation to incentives benefits, those same legal structures tell us more. They also tell us a lot about what that particular society believes its incentive needs are, in comparison to how great its inequality moral costs are. And here, different societies will differ both from each other and in different circumstances. Recalling World War II rationing is helpful to understanding this. During that period of total war, and for the limited time of that war, two things were true. First, an incentive-based economic system seemed of little importance. For the duration of the war, direct command seemed preferable. Second, in total war, equality values run especially strong.[7] Little wonder, then, that in such a war a huge number of goods were treated as merit goods and were removed from the ordinary market. A society's particular decision as to what the (sadly short-lived) great economist Arthur Okun called the "great trade-off"[8] can be criticized. Whether the exact trade-off is the right one for a particular time must always be open for discussion. But the existence of such an often implicit decision, and its effect on the legal structure of a society and on that society's actual treatment of various merit goods, cannot be denied.

B.

One more point needs to be emphasized before I close this essay by returning to certain specific merit goods in order to suggest what their treatment shows about the benefits and costs of various ways of treating such goods in general. This is that the nonordinary market treatment of *some* goods is, in fact, probably essential to the perdurance of incentives! It is often asserted that a society's equality desires are best met by a generalized reduction of wealth differences and not by the treatment of some goods as outside the general market.[9] It is certainly possible that if the only decision available were "what *general* wealth distribution should a society have?," the distribution that would be chosen would be so egalitarian that incentives would be significantly limited. But it is also possible that if the question were—what, in fact, it is—"what general wealth distributions should a society have, *if certain specific goods and bads are removed from allocation by that wealth distribution?*," the distribution that would result would be one that allowed much play for incentives. In other words, the recognition of merit goods and their extraction from the ordinary allocation system can result in the acceptance of a significantly more inegalitarian wealth distribution than would obtain if no merit goods were recognized. And, I dare say, this is precisely what our existing legal structures suggest is the case.[10]

For this reason, I would argue that those very people who believe in the importance of incentives in our society, rather than decrying the nonmarket treatment of some goods, might be well advised to welcome that treatment. To put it another way, in a truly socialist—that is, wealth distribution–egalitarian, non-incentive-based—society, merit goods of this sort would scarcely exist. Some goods might still be allocated in uncommon ways to avoid inequalities of power. And those goods whose commandification, no less than their commodification, was unacceptable would demand special treatment. But the importance and variety of goods that got "merit" treatment would be small in comparison to that which obtains in a free enterprise society. In this sense, the existence of such goods is essential to free enterprise, given the ambivalence between equality and incentives that pervades most free enterprise societies!

C.

Let us now look more specifically at goods that are today widely treated as merit goods, and consider what their treatment tells us about the varied means that are available to us for allocating them. And let us also, and especially importantly, examine what their treatment reveals about the relationship between the two categories of merit goods that I have been discussing—those that demand nonordinary market treatment to avoid the costs of commodification, and those that call for that treatment to avoid undue dependency on the prevailing wealth distribution.

The current treatment of primary and secondary education in the United States is a useful place to start. First, the existence, importance, and general acceptance of private, openly priced education is strong evidence that as to this merit good society's concerns do not arise primarily from its being priced. And the fact that, with virtually no objections, education is made broadly mandatory indicates that direct and open command is also not a problem. Neither commodification costs nor commandification ones are of particular importance here. But what is as significant is the degree of agreement that, at least at a minimal level, this good should be available to all equally, and not purchased even in a subsidized market. At first glance, then, it would seem that, up to a certain level of education, individual choices are deemed unimportant, and collective allocation can, without more, be used.[11] However, whether that commanded allocation of education is, in fact, equal is anything but clear. And this is so as to most of our multiple federalist sovereignties. Who gets assigned to what school, and how capable many such schools are of delivering even minimum levels of the relevant good, are surely controversial. But, allegedly, the allocation of education is made collectively and equally.

Beyond that minimal level, though, the pure wealth-dependent market could be said to dominate. Both at the lower school levels, where private, superior (or so the private schools claim) education can be bought, and at the higher levels, where almost all education is fee-based, the ordinary market seems to rule. In fact, however, the matter is much more complex. To the extent that *public* higher education is made available to many at a below-market price, higher education can be viewed as being furnished through a tax/subsidy scheme that mitigates significantly the effects of the underlying wealth distribution. And, even at the lower educational levels, some—much more than minimal—education is given to those who qualify for special, or magnet schools. Collective decisions apply, are legion, and result in the allocation of a greater amount of the good to those admitted to such schools. Such subsidized special schools deliver an educational product in competition with and separate from what can be bought from private schools.

In addition, even the privately provided good is not assigned solely through a wealth distribution–dependent market. The fact that society's desire for altruism can be, and is, satisfied in this area in important ways,[12] means that top-level education is given to some in direct opposition to the prevailing distribution of wealth.[13] Need-based scholarships make more than minimal levels of this good available to the poor. They do not create a fully wealth distribution–neutral market by any means. But they do go some distance in that direction.[14]

Finally, recent voucher and charter school developments suggest, dramatically I think, that any supposed minimum level of equality is far from totally acceptable if it does not recognize different views as to how the minimum should be provided. The matter is subject to considerable current controversy. And as is often the case, the degree to which the controversy reflects the distributional interests of particular groups can be argued.[15] But the fact that voucher systems and charter schools enjoy considerable popular support is powerful evidence that some, at least, would prefer a modified market method of allocating the minimal amount of education that is given free instead of the traditional command-ordained, formal equality approach that seemed to dominate for years. And interestingly, the modified market approach employed is one that looks a lot like those used in wartime rationing.[16]

Seen in its full reality, the allocation of education is a prime example of the multiple approaches available for the allocation of merit goods and of their complex interactions. Because neither commodification nor commandification is a problem, however, it does not give us much insight into what is done when a good is considered to be of merit for both of the reasons I have described. What it does show, though, is how the allocation of a crucially important good is, with relatively little controversy, deemed best removed from the full influence of the prevailing wealth distribution, rather than being determined by potentially dramatic alterations in that distribution.[17]

D.

Health and medical care is a useful agglomeration of merit goods to examine, for both its similarity to and its differences from education. Here, too, there is in most Western societies a general agreement that a minimum amount of health care should be removed from the ordinary market. And this view, never absent for some members of our society,[18] seems to be taking hold even in the United States. In health care—as in education—the systems that have been established have been extraordinarily complex mixtures of direct command, equalizations of the market through tax and subsidy, reductions of the influence of pure market wealth dependence accomplished through private altruism, and even rationing. Our approach to health care is so complex, in fact, that even just outlining it in any detail falls well beyond this book's scope. But two things are worth noting.

First, the weight that should be given to individual choices and desires, even with respect to the minimum amount of the good that is made generally available, has from the start been crucial to the health debate. This is in sharp contrast to education, where this element has, only relatively recently, become a central part of the discussion. Finding ways of letting people express individual desires, both because people badly want to express those desires, and because the costs of any system that allows them to express those desires are very significant, has been crucial to the health debate from its inception and has also been responsible for many of its difficulties. This has been so as well with respect to the minimum amount of health care that should be made available.

Second, in contrast to education, both commodification and commandification appear to be significant problems. The whole discussion of death panels, twisted and politically motivated though it may have been, is directly on point.[19] The claim that such panels were part of President Barack Obama's health plan resonated politically, precisely because these panels were made to look like the kind of collective life-and-death decisions that people object to: command decisions that give rise to significant moral costs. The debate on these panels centered on collectively made life-and-death decisions. But not far from the discussion was also the fear that life and death might be being given a market price.

How strong the objections to—in other words, how great the costs of—commandification and commodification are in this area, I cannot say. It is enough, for now, to point out their existence and to note that their presence is an important part of the reasons for the differences in the education and health care debates. Unlike in education, whatever approaches are ultimately established in the health care field must come to terms with the need to reduce the costs of obvious commodification and of obvious commandification.

E.

Allocations of child rights and of transplantable body parts involve areas where, traditionally, commodification and commandification costs have seemed very high. And this may explain why, as discussed in *Tragic Choices*, these merit goods have been the subjects of complicated subterfuges designed to make plausible the assertion that neither price-based nor direct-collective allocations have occurred, although they obviously have. But I am far from sure that, at least as to some body parts, whatever commodification/commandification costs currently adhere to them, these would remain significant were a predominantly wealth distribution–neutral, tax/subsidy-based market made available. Both of these merit goods and various approaches to distributing them have been discussed at length in *Tragic Choices*, and I will not repeat that discussion here.[20] But I would be surprised, were a relatively wealth-neutral system put in place, if we would find strong objection to the existence of market prices on blood, corneas, bone marrows, and perhaps even kidneys and livers.[21] This is especially so if the availability of these from cadavers as well as live donors is part of the market. Some things, like semen and ova—body parts that one might think are more linked to an individual's personhood—would seem to entail greater problems of pricing and commodification. But the existence today of ordinary and legal markets in these suggests that personhood is less important than is the fact that these items can broadly and easily be recreated by the donor. This fact seems to be more important in diminishing external moral costs than any dislike of one's gene pool being priced.

F.

I have already discussed military service in outlining possible treatments of those merit goods that arise in reaction to their dependence on the prevailing wealth distribution. And military service was one of the examples analyzed at length in *Tragic Choices.* Not much more needs to be said. The lack of any significant commodification objection is interesting. (Paying what could be viewed as a "body price" for some volunteers has always been part of selective service.) As is the fact that commandification objections have long been present here. Moreover, though they have been overridden in various of our wars,[22] commandification concerns remain extremely strong, both as to who should be drafted at all and as to who should be assigned to the most life-threatening tasks and areas.[23] Together, especially when combined with the additional fact that individual differences in desire to serve and in abhorrence of service in the military are very great, these facts suggest that selective service might well be a prime place for a relatively wealth distribution–neutral market to prevail.

As described earlier, either a somewhat neutral market of the rationing or of the tax/subsidy sort could fairly easily be established. And, from time to time, both have been suggested. That neither has been adopted is itself enlightening. It may be that this is because the very advantages of such relatively neutral markets— that they would give important information as to the desirability or abhorrence of a particular war—are too costly collectively. A relatively reliable set of market votes that show that a war, which the holders of collective power want to enter, is deeply unpopular may be just the kind of data that those in power do not wish to hear, and hence they are willing to impose significant costs on the society in order to avert that data being made available.

G.

And so I turn to the last of the merit goods I have been concerned with that have demonstrably been treated as such in our society. This is the right to influence election results by making either campaign contributions or expenditures. The most important thing to note about this merit good is that it is currently the subject of a prolonged and deep debate between popularly elected legislatures and the U.S. Supreme Court. The High Court, in the face of what many elected legislatures had established, has declared that treating the right to spend money to influence elections on the basis of the prevailing wealth distribution is close to a constitutional requirement. And the treatment of campaign expenditure as a wealth disproportion–based merit good has been held, in a variety of contexts, to be *unconstitutional!* The Court has, from time to time, adverted to the power-based distributional dangers of letting elected legislatures limit the wealth dependence of campaign contributions. They have noted that laws regulating campaign funds too readily can be used to benefit incumbents. And this would be a typical use of a merit good rationale to benefit a *power*-ful interest group distributionally. It would be a shift from market allocations to power allocations in order to benefit those who hold the greater amount of power. But since the Supreme Court allows campaign finance regulations on grounds other than the desire to level the economic playing field, such as to avoid corruption, and since anti-corruption-grounded campaign finance regulations can also be written so as to benefit incumbents, this is not likely the reason for the Court's constitutional attack on campaign expenditure as a merit good.[24] Court control of incumbent legislators' attempts to move from market-based distributions to power-based ones may well be needed. But, to the extent it is, it should be applied also, and as effectively, to regulations centered on corruption as to those designed to counter wealth disproportions.

Why, then, has the Court taken the remarkable position that it is unconstitutional to treat campaign expenditures as a wealth disproportion–based merit good? Some have asserted that the Court's stand is itself distributional: a desire to benefit and increase the power of the rich and of whatever political party they adhere to.[25] That is not for me even to consider since, being a judge, any such assertion would not be a proper one for me to make. As a judge, what I can do—and indeed have done[26]—is to examine and question the legal-constitutional basis of what, to date, remains, albeit by a bare majority, the absolute position taken by the Court.

As a scholar, however, I am less interested in the Court's holding than I am in the fact that it flies in the face of pretty clear popular desires. In other words, as a scholar what concerns me is the fact that what the Court seems to be constitutionally ordaining imposes significant external moral (and perhaps also traditional economic) costs on people. And these are costs that the bearers have sought, through legislative action, to avoid.[27]

That our Constitution can, and often does, impose costs that a majority of people would rather not bear is certainly the case. Moreover, it is surely the duty of the Supreme Court to impose such costs when that is so. But what has often been stated by constitutional law scholars is true here as well: if those costs are great, and the majority does not like to bear them, then the High Court had better be very sure that the basis of its decision lies in the Constitution.[28] Antimajoritarian rulings made to protect historically disadvantaged groups frequently have had such strong bases.[29] Antimajoritarian rulings that do not protect such minorities are harder to justify.[30]

Be that as it may, were campaign expenditures permitted by the High Court to be treated as a wealth disproportion–based merit good, market mechanisms to deal with them could be easily described. Indeed, before the Supreme Court's intervention many such approaches were legislatively established. This is partly because campaign expenditures are in no way prone to commodification costs—they involve money and a commodity, elected office, that is normally acceptably influenced through both money and power. It is also because those collective controls that do not work through markets are frequently suspect in this area. Costs akin to those of commandification—linked to the protection of, and increase in, the power of those who disproportionately have the power that incumbents hold—adhere to campaign expenditure regulations. The result is that campaign expenditures would seem to be prime subjects for tax/subsidy market modifications, were the Supreme Court but to allow them.

These could range from (a) relatively minor subsidizations (through government matches of the contributions of the poor) or similarly small taxations of the contributions of the rich, to (b) the establishment of a full wealth distribution–neutral market of the sort described earlier. The rich would be taxed substantially on whatever political contributions or expenditures they made, and the funds so raised could be used to multiply the campaign expenditures and contributions of the poor.[31] In between lie the many and varied matching and limiting programs enacted by legislatures in the past. Some of these may infringe more than others on the constitutional values that the High Court has asserted are involved.[32] But, absent a judicial constitutional prohibition, one would expect that a tax/subsidy approach could be found that, relatively easily, attenuated wealth differences in the allocation of this extremely important merit good to a degree deemed optimal by a particular legislature.

H.

What, then, does this examination of merit goods tell us about the demands that the lawyer-economist must make on economic theory? What, apart from some suggestions for further study of these goods, can we derive from the above discussion? It seems to me that there are three points to be made. And, interestingly, they are points that can also be made with respect to my forthcoming discussion of altruism.

The first is the importance of the availability and usefulness of modified markets and modified command structures. One cannot understand societies' treatment of merit goods without understanding the role of modified methods—both market and command. The second, though also relevant to altruism, is more relevant to a still later essay. It is that the uses of command and of market mechanisms to achieve the goals of a given society are far more complex and intertwined than is usually considered in economic models or even in discussions by lawyer-economists. The third is that traditional economic theorists have too often ignored, or treated as nonexistent, irrational, or not worth considering, costs and values that people in the world deem very real indeed.[33] These values and tastes that people hold—like some analogous costs that people believe they are made to bear and would like to see diminished—crucially affect both the private behaviors and the legal structures that are evident in most societies' treatment of merit goods.[34] As we shall soon see, they are also the reason for the prevalence of various forms of altruism, beneficence, and not-for-profit institutions. But, as we shall see in the last essays in this book, and as is especially important for my present project, they demand consideration (a) of the positions economists do, in fact, take all the time with respect to tastes and values, (b) of how such positions should be more openly discussed and analyzed, and, most important of all, (c) of what economists can do, better than anyone else, to help lawmakers and legal scholars come to intelligent decisions about the shaping of tastes and values.

V

Of Altruism, Beneficence, and Not-for-Profit Institutions

A.

Many economists, when they discuss altruism, look at it only as a means. They ask whether altruistic behavior or beneficence is an efficient way of getting something done. They examine whether not-for-profit institutions deliver a particular good or service as cheaply as self-interested ones. And the answer to these questions is most frequently no.[1] There may be some discussion of the quality of the service that is being delivered. Is the education given by not-for-profit schools the same as that furnished by for-profit ones? Is the medical care given by not-for-profit hospitals different from that given by for-profit ones?[2] But in the end, the question asked remains the same: If people want a good—medical care, education, or whatever—is beneficence or self-interest the cheapest way of producing it?[3]

The frequent conclusion that self-interest gets us what we want more cheaply (even allowing for some differences in the final product) presents us with a typical Law and Economics problem of the sort I discussed earlier. If self-interest is more effective at producing the goods we want, why do we, *in fact,* have so much altruism, so much beneficence, and so many not-for-profit structures in the world? When faced with this question, many scholars have not reacted as Coase did when he faced the reality of the existence of firms. They have, instead, looked to complicated historical, evolutionary, or egotistical explanations for what, in a fundamental sense, struck them as bizarre.[4]

All this seems to me to be more than "passing strange!" My own reaction to the perdurance of altruism and not-for-profits is that they must be there not simply as means to an end but because we like them. We have beneficence because we want it and are willing to pay for it. Thus, altruism and beneficence can readily be viewed as ends in themselves; they can be seen as things we have in our utility functions. So viewed, they need no more to be explained by economists than would any other taste or value. I will, later in this book, discuss what I think is a paradoxical attitude in traditional economic theory toward tastes and values. I will argue that economists, on the one hand, frequently assume without analysis the worthiness of some and the uselessness of other values, and that, on the other hand, they do not do what they are supremely qualified to do. That is, they do not help us analyze why in many circumstances, and on quite simple assumptions, some tastes and values are, *in fact,* preferable (in an *economic* sense) to others. But that is for later; in this essay I will stay with the traditional position that economists have nothing to say as to tastes and values.[5]

Once beneficence is viewed as an end in itself—as a good we desire, as something in our utility functions—the fact that it may be an expensive taste should not be a problem. It is—in this sense—as foolish to ask whether altruism or self-interest is a cheaper way of being educated or giving medical care as it is to ask whether eating potatoes or caviar is a cheaper way of being fed. It makes no more sense, if we want not-for-profits because we "like" beneficence, to ask whether not-for-profits "efficiently" bring about the production/achievement of some other good than it does to question whether we quench our thirst more "efficiently" with plain water or fine Burgundy wine, whether it would be more effective to procreate through sperm collecting farms (as is done for cattle) or by making love. We do what we do, even if it costs more, because we like it and are willing to pay that price.

It may, of course, be well worth examining how high the price of the good we want actually is, and then studying how much we really do prefer the costlier good. But the mere existence of an expensive good *as an end* that shapes our behavior should not be, for the economist, a problem. It should not be seen as an irrationality that needs complex explanations or merits disapproval. Why, then, is it that beneficence and its cousins are so frequently treated that way?

A possible reason is both interesting in itself and has—as I hope to show—some significance for economic theory generally. It stems from what I call McKean's paradox, named after Roland McKean, the Virginia economist who, years ago, stated the problem. McKean said that it is meaningless to ask, "How much must I offer you to get you to love me for myself quite apart from my offer?"[6] In other words, if we treat altruism or beneficence as an ordinary good, and try to buy it in the market rather than increasing the amount of it that is produced, as occurs with most goods, we destroy it.

And, significantly, it is equally meaningless to ask, "How can I compel you to love me, for myself alone?" That is, just as use of a pure market destroys the good it seeks to increase, so too does pure command! It would seem, then, that the two canonical ways in economic theory for optimizing production of a good both fail, and may even destroy the good in question. I cannot say for sure whether this is the reason beneficence and its cousins are rarely treated as ends in much economic analysis. But it seems plausible to me. And once the issue is put this way, quite a few interesting things follow.

While it is true that I may not be able to get you to love me for myself alone by purchasing your love in a pure market . . . candy helps! And while it may be true that I cannot command you to be beneficent without destroying the beneficence that I value and desire, education—a mighty powerful form of command—may bring about just the result I want.[7] In other words, pure markets and pure commands may not achieve our goals—indeed, may be counterproductive—if the goods we desire are things like altruism and beneficence. But that does not mean that through complex modified markets, and less direct and less centralized command structures, we may not be able to do—as to these goods—what we do through traditional markets and command for most goods.[8]

It might be argued, however, that there is no need to consider altruism as a good in itself because individuals can satisfy their desire for that good simply by being altruistic themselves.[9] This, however, is not an adequate explanation. It does not deal with the likely fact that individuals also desire state beneficence; that state beneficence, also, is a good in our utility functions. And, more important, it assumes (incorrectly I think) that as to private beneficence, the desire—what I am assuming is in our utility functions—can be satisfied by *my* acting altruistically. While such (literally) "self-satisfying" behavior may help, somewhat, what individuals may well desire most (what they are willing to pay a price for) is beneficence by others, that is, altruistic behavior generally.

Indeed, as we shall see later in this essay, beneficence and altruism are not *one* good that we have a desire for, but a group of interrelated, only partly substitutable goods, and that we wish to optimize the amount of each such good in relation to the others.[10] Rather than ignoring the reality that these goods are ones that we want, that we have in our utility functions, we should, therefore, examine what kinds of modified markets and modified command structures are most effective in optimizing the production of goods of this sort.

This way of looking at the problem has important consequences not simply for altruism and beneficence, but also for economic theory generally. Let me explore the latter briefly, before returning to altruism, beneficence, and the existence of not-for-profit institutions, and what happens when we talk about them as ends and not means.

B.

The moment we realize that, in the world as it is, we use multiple forms of modified markets and modified command structures to increase/encourage the amount of altruism and beneficence that is produced, we also realize (a) that these are not the only goods and bads as to which modified markets and commands are more effective tools for optimization than pure ones would be, and (b) that the market and command structures that are, in fact, used in the economy are enormously more complicated than is usually posited.

Looking at this second insight first, in Coasean terms, the relative costs to be compared are not the cost of using "The Market" as against the cost of using "Command"; they are, instead,

the costs of using any one of many modifications of each in relation to each other. Indeed, this can clearly be seen in Coase's
earliest work. Coase, in "The Nature of the Firm," noted that the
existence of firms demonstrated that, in contexts where they were
found, the cost of command was less than the cost of market
relationships.[11] But the command structure he was contrasting to
his newly posited costly markets was not a classic centralized
governmental command structure. What he was comparing with
market relationships was the highly decentralized, private command structure that characterizes relationships within firms. It
was this *modified* command structure that won out over contractual market relationships. If pure, centralized governmental
command were the only alternative, who is to say whether that
command relationship would, in fact, be more efficient in achieving what Coase's firms sought to accomplish than would some
form of market.

Indeed, and as always, Coase was more nuanced and far-
seeing than many of those who followed him. First, he saw and
briefly discussed whether some might prefer a command structure to a market structure, even if the former were more costly.
That is, he was willing to do, with respect to firm structures,
what I have suggested relatively few do with respect to beneficence and altruism: to consider command structures as goods
in themselves.[12] I'll have more to say about this later when I
discuss the relationship between markets and command in the
liability rule. Second, he was well aware of the fact that the
command structure he was talking about in "The Nature of the
Firm" was not fixed, but would fluctuate as entrepreneurs ex-
perimented with governing different aspects of their business
through command within the firm or through contract in the
market.[13] The complexity of the firm command structure and
command structures generally has also been noted by such

distinguished scholars as Alchian, Demsetz, Williamson, and Holmstrom.[14]

If, in fact, one looks at the world of firms as they actually are (as Law and Economics in my view demands one should), one finds a typically complex scene. Occasionally, centralized command—government "firms"—win out. Frequently, private, decentralized command structures—ordinary firms—dominate. And, from time to time, modified markets—complex, contractual arrangements—rule. And this complexity is not limited to the use of modified command and markets in the area of firms.[15]

My point is this. An examination of altruism as an end has led me to question the existence of only pure markets and only pure command structures.[16] It also leads me to say that, in fact, our legal–economic world is full of much more complicated modified market and modified command structures than one might, at first, imagine. This is a fact with significance going well beyond any discussion of altruism, of firms, or, indeed, of merit goods. It is true, as I'll say soon enough, that one cannot discuss altruism intelligently without being conscious of these modified market and modified command structures. But it is also true that the existence of these modified structures is important in any number of other areas as well. And we would be well advised to take them into account, to analyze them and to study their significance in and of themselves *and in relation to each other.* That is, we need to do this, not only as has elegantly been done with respect to modified command structures,[17] but also as to modified markets *and* with respect to the interplay of the two.

What are the goods for which modified structures abound? What characterizes them? Do they have things in common? When do they predominate? All these questions are worth study.

Philip Bobbitt and I, in *Tragic Choices,*[18] examined some such goods—and bads—though not as systematically as I am now suggesting is appropriate. That is, we looked at them through the eyes of the *lawyer*-economist. I did some of the same when I discussed merit goods earlier in this book. What I am suggesting now, however, is that just as the discussion of altruism has, it seems to me, called for an examination and analysis of the multiple *forms* of modified markets and modified command structures that exist, so too does that same discussion call for a systematic treatment of the wide variety of goods and bads that, in our societies, seem best dealt with not by pure markets or commands, but by complex variations and mixtures of these.

That is not my job today. The job of the lawyer-economist is to suggest that sometimes economic theory needs to be amplified to explain what *is* the legal world. Examining the significance of that amplification and analyzing it further are frequently the jobs of the economist. When Coase said that one couldn't explain the existence of firms without positing that markets are costly, he was making an important institutionalist point. The ultimate analysis and significance of that point, of the fact that markets are costly, and what *that* meant for economics generally, was a matter to be dealt with by *economic theorists*. And, in time, it was, and very well indeed!

That said, I return to a discussion of altruism, beneficence, and not-for-profits. My aim, let me repeat, is not a full treatment of these issues, or anything close to one. Lord knows, there is already in being a huge and often excellent literature dealing with them.[19] What I mean to do, once again, is to look at the legal world, and from that "look" to raise some questions for further economic analysis. I will concentrate on three issues. First, are altruism and its cousins one single good, or are they, as I will assert, several different goods that we desire? Second, what means have actually been used to optimize these different goods, and why? And third, what indications do we have as to the "price" we are willing to pay for these goods and hence as to how much of these goods we want? In other words, if altruism and its cousins are like caviar and truffles, how much caviar and truffles, as against potatoes, do we wish to have?

C.

Once one treats altruism and its cousins as something we want, and are willing to pay for, it becomes immediately evident that what we want is not just one good, but a collection of goods. Each of these goods can serve as a more or less expensive means to a particular end (and hence they can, in some sense, substitute for each other as "means"). But each of them also has some *individual* characteristics that we want, that are ends in and of themselves. Still, even these individual characteristics themselves are of a sort that can, to some extent, be substituted for. As a result, the group of goods we are concerned with are, to some degree, substitutes for each other, not only as means but also as ends.

Let me be specific. I believe that it is hard to look at the world of legal institutions and relationships and not conclude that people want altruism in a variety of forms and that, while each form may be a substitute for another, both as means and as ends, they are, like most goods, less than perfect substitutes. People want other people to behave beneficently, and in altruistic ways toward them. They are willing to pay a fair amount to be in contact with each other in ways that are seemingly not self-interested. As a result, they establish such relationships even though that "contact" could often be accomplished more cheaply through self-interest. But even if everyone behaved altruistically toward others in the private sphere, people would be unhappy if their government were not also charitable and beneficent, at least to some extent. That is, a thousand private charities are not enough. People want private beneficence *and* public beneficence, too. And that is why a "cradle to grave" beneficent government—which as a *means* might well result in everyone being well cared for—would also not satisfy fully. It would not be a completely adequate substitute for private beneficence. A world in which people were all self-seeking and brutish, but the government was totally loving, would be as unsatisfactory as a world in which people were all loving and caring, but the state was harsh and mean.

What is more, even if the state and individuals were optimally caring (that is, optimally satisfied the desire for private *and* public beneficence), people would probably also want private firms to be, to some degree, altruistic. This is indicated by the perdurance of not-for-profit firms. But it is also shown, perhaps more dramatically, in the returns that for-profit institutions clearly derive from their occasional altruistic behavior.[20]

Altruism, then, is not just caviar; it is not just a fine Burgundy wine. It is a collection of goods that can substitute for each other as *means,* but also that are each wanted as different ends in themselves.[21] But as ends, too, they substitute for each other to some extent. Altruism in its various forms is caviar *and* truffles *and* porcini mushrooms; it is Burgundy, Barolo, and a truly good beer. Each of these serves to satisfy our hunger and our thirst. In this sense, they are all means and can—according to their prices—substitute for each other as ways of achieving that "feeding" end. But, in addition, they each serve to satisfy a *different* epicurean desire for fineness in dining and drinking. In this respect also, they can to some degree be substitutes for each other. We would not be satisfied by, indeed we would tire of, a diet that sought to meet our hunger and fine dining requirements by giving us only one of these. Unlimited caviar and few truffles is less satisfying than a decent amount of each![22] The same is true of the various forms of altruism and beneficence.

Governments, private individuals, and firms each can, in brutish or in altruistic fashion, take care of our educational and health needs. In this sense, altruism and self-interest can substitute for each other as means. And, in response to the cost of each, we can choose altruistic or self-interested ways of achieving these educational and health care ends. But we also choose how much of each of these health care and educational ends we wish to have satisfied by private altruism and by private self-seeking, by state beneficence and by harsh state command, by profit and by not-for-profit firm behavior. We do this on the basis of how much of each kind of altruistic behavior we desire as an end in itself. The complex mixture we come up with should be that combination of different goods which will (a) get us to the ends (health care, education) we want, but also (b) respond to our desire for the different goods, the different "means," as ends in themselves. We seek the way that gets us our optimal mix of these goods as ends, while also using these goods as means to other ends. *And we want the combination that achieves both most efficiently.* Moreover, we want that combination to take into account that different people value these goods, even as ends, differently. Some of us care enormously about beneficence generally; others don't. And some care a lot about private beneficence and little about state altruism, while others, instead, reverse that valuation.

Thus, like different fine drinks *and* plain water, like caviar, truffles, porcini, *and* potatoes, we want a combination of state, private, and firm beneficence that gives us the health care and education that we want (that feeds and quenches us), and at the same time satisfies optimally our desire for, and joy in, seeing people, governments, and firms behave "nicely" (that satisfies our delight in sating our hunger and our thirst, sometimes with one and sometimes with another of these fine foods and wines). And we want a combination that recognizes that we vary in our desire for health care and education, and in the value we give to altruistic behavior by states, firms, and individuals—that some among us are thirstier than others, and that some much prefer pinot noir to claret.

The multifarious nature (and potential substitutability, at two levels, as ends and as means) of altruism and beneficence presents particular challenges for economic analysis. Specifically, the questions I just posed all go to the difficulty of optimizing the production of somewhat substitutable goods that are both ends and means and as to which neither pure markets nor pure command structures work at all well. These questions, which are fundamental ones for any welfare economic analysis that hopes to speak relevantly to the world of real legal relationships, are what I hope economic theorists will, in time, help us address. I certainly cannot do that in this book. But I do hope that a bit more discussion of altruism can give insights into the problems that the questions pose and hence how we can to try to move toward answers.

The legal scholars, the institutionalists who look at legal structures (far more carefully than I can here) would immediately discern that there are some areas of human need where the "need" is almost always met by self-interested relationships and some, instead, where a considerable (and in some areas almost total) amount of altruistic relationships predominate. Such a scholar would also find that in some of these areas that altruistic relationship is largely governmental, in others largely individual, and in still others significantly in the control of not-for-profit firms. That suggests that if the *good* is the differing desire, by different people, of different amounts of public, private, and firm beneficence, that good is produced most efficiently when one takes into account the comparative advantage that states, private individuals, and not-for-profit firms have in producing the *ends* that good also seeks to achieve. Moreover, this comparative advantage relates both to the desire by individuals to *have* altruistic state, private, and firm behavior, and their desire to *obtain,* say, good health care, education, or bananas relatively cheaply. (Or, to put it another way, it asks how comparatively good caviar, truffles, and porcini *are* at feeding us, in relation to potatoes, and what combination of these delicacies meets the desires of our varied taste buds best—given the different costs of each—compared both to each other and to potatoes, and accounting for the fact that some of us prefer caviar and others porcini.)

This way of looking at the problem ought, I think, to lead to studies that tell us much more than we now know about the concentration of altruistic structures—state, individual, and firms—in certain areas, and the difference within these areas as to which of the different altruistic forms—state, individual, and not-for-profit firms—predominate. Why is it that altruistic behavior is relatively unimportant in the production and distribution of shoes and bananas and very significant in health and education? It is not simply that the *cost* of altruism as against self-interest is less in some areas than in others. Nor is it only that the product (what is *produced*) in some of these areas may be viewed as somewhat different if the producer is altruistic or self-interested (and perhaps in some sense a better product, even if costlier). It may also be that the altruism demonstrated in the production of different goods is more desired than that demonstrated in the production of other goods. We might get more pleasure from altruistic behavior that leads to health care than altruistic behavior that leads to shoes. Why? Again, simply because that is what our tastes are! We might, in other words, get more pleasure from the same good wine if we drank it at dinner with someone we love than if we consumed it alone in the middle of the day.[23]

Similarly, even in those areas where altruism as a means is a relatively efficient way of producing a product and, in itself, a relatively effective response to the desire for altruism as an end, there are—I think it cannot be disputed—significant differences in the comparative effectiveness, both as means and as ends, of altruistic governments, private relationships, and private firms. Which altruistic "producer" gets the most altruistic bang for the buck differs with the different products that altruism as a means seeks to provide. A careful set of empirical studies looking—from this point of view—at how, in fact, altruistic relationships are spread across the legal landscape— where they are dominant, where occasional, and where virtually nonexistent—and looking also at what different forms of altruism (private, state, and firm) predominate, are rare, or are virtually nonexistent, would tell us a great deal about beneficence and its cousins. It would also tell us a lot about how, as society and technology change, we might reform those relationships and structures in response to new comparative advantages.

But it might also tell us more. It might tell us about how the predominance of altruism in some but not in other areas is itself a response to the two remaining questions that I wish to pose in this essay with respect to altruism:

i. How do we get an optimal amount and mix of altruism? What modified command and market incentives can we use to achieve most effectively the production of the amount and sort of altruistic behavior we want? Just as we should seek to determine where altruism works best (in the production of health care, say, rather than bananas), and when some form of beneficence (private, say, versus state) is most effective, so, through empirical studies like those suggested above, we could try to learn what modified markets and modified command methods work best, and where. Such studies, moreover, might guide us to a fuller theory of the broad range of and interrelationships among semi-, hemi-, demi-markets and commands that I believe is essential to welfare economics.

ii. How, in this area, where the pure market and pure command approaches do not work, can we get from modified markets and modified commands the guidance we need to determine how much of complex goods like altruism and its cousins is wanted—in what areas, and through what private, state, and firm relationships? How, in other words, do we get, as to altruistic behavior and structures, data that the market in caviar, truffles, porcini mushrooms, and potatoes, or the command decision as to these, give us virtually automatically? To put it most bluntly: How can we decide how much we want to spend to get what amounts and what forms of altruism and beneficence?[24]

D.

The question of how we create incentives to produce goods that are destroyed or damaged when traditional market or command structures are employed goes well beyond the area of altruism. For, as Philip Bobbitt and I discussed in our book *Tragic Choices,* and as I considered somewhat in my chapters on merit goods in this book, such goods are many and varied.[25] Nevertheless, the experience our society has had with incentives in the area of altruism can provide some hints for these other areas as well.

Private, individual altruism can—as we see if we but look around us—be increased by a variety of indirect market-like means, each of which deserves more study. The role of gifts as a way of breaking McKean's paradox, as a way of getting someone to love me for myself alone, is the most obvious. The point is not only to induce (not buy) love, but also to induce (through rewards that have value) beneficent private behavior. At what point do the "gifts" become so clearly transactional, however, that the behavior they induce is no longer viewed as altruistic, but crass? That is the key question.

The answer lies both in the nature of the gift and in the nature of the relationship between the creator of the gift and its recipient. Giving someone even valuable gifts as signs of affection may result in returned affection and affectionate behavior. But it can become, and bespeak, a quite different relationship when the gifts become too close to, or indeed are, tit-for-tat exchanges. The relationships that then ensue carry with them their own set of pejorative terms, in part, perhaps, to distinguish them from the valuable and desired ones, pejorative terms that are employed to separate such "purchasing gifts" from those that succeed in enhancing the kind of altruistic behavior we seek to increase.[26]

But, interestingly, even transactional "gift" giving *can* help create behavior that is viewed as altruistic. It can do this especially if the relationship between donor and donee is sufficiently attenuated so that the "gift" serves to create a generic culture of altruism rather than to buy altruistic behavior directly. The prime example of this is tax deductions.[27] Were we to pay X directly to give money to a charity, we might make the charity richer, but we surely would not feel that the donation by X was altruistic. And yet it is hard to doubt that people's desire for, and pleasure from, altruistic behavior is to some degree satisfied by observing the mass of charitable donations which exist in our society and which qualify for tax deductions. Why is that?

In part, this is because while some of the charitable gift ultimately achieves a reduction in taxes, some does not. The *cost* of the altruistic behavior is reduced, and hence the underlying individual desire to help the charity made more effective and more likely to occur, but some charitable desire, some altruistic behavior was there and did manifest itself in the donation made. This element of tax deductions is, I think, akin to the effectiveness of the matching gift phenomenon. How often, on National Public Radio, say, do we hear, "If you give today, your gift will be matched by X or Y"? Its common use bespeaks its effectiveness in encouraging gifts, and yet those gifts do satisfy our pleasure in seeing altruistic behavior. Indeed, that pleasure does not seem to be much reduced by the existence of a match. We hear of "Lucy in Woodbridge, and Flaubert in Wallingford making a gift," and smile happily, and not less, because the Pincus Corporation is matching those gifts "if they are made in this hour."

But there is something else, apart from the reduction of the real cost of the sought-for altruistic behavior, that allows indirect money incentives to increase what are perceived to be beneficent actions. Even tax credits (100 percent coverage) may ultimately result in behavior that helps to satisfy our desire for altruism. This is because, to the extent that money payments have changed the culture rather than simply brought about specific donations, the charitable acts that result can satisfy our desires for altruism. It is said that the existence of tax donations, and occasionally credits, has made America and Americans *culturally* much more supportive of charities than Europeans.[28] To the degree that that is so, it should not be surprising that the charitable donations that occur here are effective in satisfying our desires for altruistic behavior.

It is often asserted that once the culture of giving is established, the elimination of the tax deduction would have little immediate effect on the amount of charitable giving.[29] The link between the money incentive and the donation has become distant and indirect. And that means that the donation both looks *and is* charitable, thereby satisfying our wish for altruistic behavior. Crucially, however, that does not mean that were the deductions eliminated, in time, charitable giving would not decline drastically. The culture would change.[30] And that is just the point: money does work, the market can increase altruism, but only when the market is not one in which money buys the good directly and immediately. It works when it changes attitudes toward giving that, for a time, become independent of the incentive.[31]

We know and see this all the time. Payments made to a particular firm (or small group of firms) to do something—whether it is job creation or use of U.S.-made products—are viewed very differently from more general payments made broadly that, in time, will create attitudes that will have the same results. Where the cutoff points are is hard to say, and whether there are more effective, more direct—collective—ways of inducing this desired behavior is always a question (as to altruism no less than as to job creation). But that indirect money payments can, like direct nonmoney gifts, lead to actions that satisfy our longing for altruistic behavior is hard to doubt.

What, then, of command incentives toward altruistic behavior? Unlike job creation, commanding that charitable actions be taken does not satisfy our desire for private altruistic behavior. Of course, it may satisfy the desire we have for a loving state, for governmental, as against private, beneficence. And, as I said earlier, that too is something that we may well wish to have. But ordering someone to be or do good, like ordering someone to love me for myself alone, does little to satisfy my longing for private love, for private goodness.

Still, there is much the collectivity can do. Command— both at the private and at the governmental level—can lead to actions in the private sphere that do satisfy our desires for altruism. A good example of this at the private-command level is the legendary Minneapolis 5 percent tradition. It is said that the old Minneapolis families, those that ran the old Minneapolis milling, lumber, and other like companies, agreed at some point (for whatever reasons) that their companies would give 5 percent of their incomes to charities.[32] In due course, it was made clear to the new arrivals, to the newly successful businesses, that their owners would only be "accepted" if their companies adhered to the same giving tradition. And so, apparently, it came to be. And now many of the donors in Minneapolis are "new" companies.

It is hard to deny that more than a few of the current donors were, to a significant degree, "commanded" to do good. And yet the tradition, the culture of giving, has sufficiently taken on a life of its own that the charitable actions of these new companies, no less than those of the old companies, do satisfy our hunger for altruism. Minneapolis is widely viewed and admired for its culture of beneficence, and the very large private donations that are manifestations of that culture make those who desire altruism feel good.[33] Not only are people fed, but they consume caviar!

In a way, this particular form of command incentivation of altruistic behavior is the exact analogue of the market incentivation represented by tax deductions. Both operate quite powerfully through self-interest to bring about, indirectly, what cannot be bought or commanded directly. The effect of both would undoubtedly continue to be felt for a considerable time even if the incentive (market or command) were eliminated. But, over a long period, the absence of the incentive might well lead to a major decline in the sought-for behavior. In other words, modified markets and commands achieve in pretty traditional ways what pure markets and commands cannot do.

And if there are also some direct (though nonmoney) market incentives, like gifts, that increase rather than destroy the sought-after "good" behavior, so there are direct command structures that do the same. If we decide, collectively, that we want people to act in certain ways (beneficently and altruistically) toward each other, we need not work only through indirect approaches. Ordering people to be good (subject to punishment if they aren't) may affect people's actions but won't satisfy the desire that people "be" good. But educating people to be good, teaching them that goodness, benevolence, etc., are virtues that individuals should appreciate and then make part of their actions, does just that.[34] When we educate individuals to be altruistic we have, in effect, chosen to command an amount of altruism, and have done so in a way that, unlike a direct order, does not undermine or destroy the good we are seeking to produce.

E.

In addition to the aforementioned modified market and modified command methods of increasing the amount of altruism that exists in our society, there is another quite remarkable market way of inducing behavior that satisfies the desire for altruism. And this is by paying—and paying very well—those who invent, create, or even simply manage altruistic structures. One example comes immediately to mind: the extraordinarily high salaries that are paid to the CEOs of certain not-for-profit firms.

Why do we pay the CEOs of not-for-profit hospitals as much as we do?[35] Many reasons for this phenomenon have been given. One can, for example, focus on the limited competition in the field that might permit such firms to earn monopoly rents, which, having nowhere else to go, can be appropriated by the charity's officers. Suggestive as some of these explanations are, they do not, it seems to me, fully explain the high pay commanded by those who run—well and successfully—not-for-profit organizations.

One possible answer suggests itself to me. To the extent that individuals value manifestations of altruism in the world of private firms—and view it as a separate, desirable good which is different from its manifestation in governmental behavior and in private interactions—one would expect that people would be willing to pay for *this* good; that they would be willing to incur some costs to get it. But how does one pay for this sort of altruism without destroying it? One way is to reward those who successfully manage not-for-profit companies that represent or manifest altruism of this sort. Indeed, even if these companies are not, in fact, very nice or altruistic, if their structure and appearance lead people to believe that they are, their existence serves to meet the demand for firm altruism and hence may justify high compensation.

One must add to the mix, however, that these companies are also there to accomplish distinct ends—e.g., to produce health care. We want them to do this relatively well (efficiently) in relation to for-profit providers who compete in seeking to achieve these same ends. Taking together the desire for altruistic behavior or the appearance of it by firms (of firm altruism as an end), and the desire for the *products* these firms produce (of firm altruism as a means, which should not be too much more expensive than self-interested means), it does not seem surprising to me that those CEOs who manage to respond well to both desires can command a special premium. They are properly in demand and are paid accordingly. They are paid well because they manage to have their firms achieve, adequately, certain results (e.g., delivery of health care), and do so without losing the appearance of having accomplished this in an altruistic, not-for-profit way.

Receiving large salaries, while at the same time seeming to further altruistic firm behavior, is not an easy act. Too often the very size of those salaries destroys the appearance of beneficence that is essential to making the not-for-profit structure be desired as an end. But, when they do not destroy that appearance, such salaries represent an almost paradigmatic modified market way of furthering the production of beneficence. They become an effective way of "paying" to give people what they seem to desire, and thereby of satisfying what is in people's utility functions.

We cannot command others to love us for ourselves alone, nor can we pay people to do that. With modifications—some small, some larger—both market and command approaches can, however, be—and in fact regularly are—used to increase the existing amount of altruistic behavior (in all *its* complexity and multiplicity of forms) that our society seems to desire, not only as a way of getting other goods but, crucially also, as an end in itself.

F.

But how can we tell how much of the various forms of altruism we want? With caviar, truffles, and porcini mushrooms, we believe (as taught by economic theory) that the market, by and large, gets us the amount, in relation *inter alia* to potatoes, that is wanted. We are, moreover, confident (again, traditional economics tells us) that collective command decisions are available to modify or substitute for that market result, should we collectively decide that the market result does not represent what is truly wanted in the caviar, truffle, porcini, . . . and potato mix. Can we, however, say the same of altruism?

The pay that is given CEOs of not-for-profits suggests that the market to some extent acts directly to affect the amount of various forms of altruistic behavior that is produced. And, of course, collective decisions, designed to encourage (or discourage) the amounts of the various forms of altruism that are extant, do represent collective determinations that respond directly to what and how much are collectively desired. The fact, moreover, that the collective decisions must be effectuated in somewhat less direct ways than are collective decisions which affect other goods makes no difference in this respect. That we must educate in order to encourage (or discourage) altruism of different sorts in no way reduces the validity of the collective decision as to how much altruism and how much of each form of it are wanted.

But can we say—with anywhere near the confidence that traditional economic theory gives us, when speaking of the market (or the market modified by collective/command actions) as producer of most goods—that the above-described modified market, modified command decisions yield us the right amount of altruism? Can we assert that the existing combination of modified market and modified command approaches yields not only the optimal *amount* of beneficence, but also the optimal *mix* of different forms of altruism, in response to a given society's wants? I have no idea.

And the reason I do not know is, I think, plausibly interesting. We have not had (and it is very hard to work out) the kind of theoretical tracking of modified markets that classical economic theory has given us as to pure markets. We do not have a model that demonstrates that, under certain conditions, an optimal result is achieved. Could such a model be formulated, and what would be its result if it were? I do not know. I do know, however, that the world the lawyer sees is filled with hemi-, semi-, demi-, and mixed types of market incentives. And, in Coasean terms, these mixed devices seem to be used because they work better—because they are in some sense more efficient—than pure market incentives. It would, therefore, be interesting to determine whether and how such modified market incentives could be integrated into a welfare economic model. It would also be interesting—and perhaps more likely to be achievable—to examine how the existence of these modified market incentives affects and modifies the results of the traditional welfare economic pure market model. And if such a complicated modified model were ever created, it would be interesting to consider what collective interventions (either by pure or by modified commands) would best complete (make most efficient) the work of this modified model.[36]

G.

All that is, obviously, beyond the scope of this essay, which seeks to show how looking at altruism through the eyes of a lawyer-economist can be fruitful. How must economic theory modify itself to explain the existence of highly varied altruistic structures and behaviors? What would the consequences of such a modified theory be for other areas of economic analysis of the world as it is? Can at least some of these modifications be incorporated into a more general economic theory? Or must they be analyzed—less rigorously I fear—by lawyers themselves? Must they be examined in an *ad hoc* fashion—with or without the aid of other social sciences—to help would-be lawmakers address what the law cannot avoid addressing; that is, to assist such lawmakers in dealing with the existence of real-world phenomena (like altruism in its varied forms) that lawmakers face when they seek to confirm, criticize, and redo the legal order? *Asking* these questions, not giving answers to them— together with the suggestion for some possible areas of further research—is what this essay is about.

It may be said, however, that the essay is fundamentally flawed because it fails to define altruism, even in a rudimentary way. Perhaps, but that failure of definition is not casual or accidental; indeed, it is a part of the analysis. If, as I have argued, altruistic structures and behaviors are *not* one good, but a whole category of things—individual, firm-centered, and governmental—that people want to see in their society, and if, moreover, people want these both as ends in themselves and as means to other ends (to the provision of other goods), then to begin by defining in some structured and precise way what these things are seems to me to be both highly arrogant and premature. We need, in other words, to learn far more about the

various forms of behavior, relationships, and structures that—
with a fair degree of substitutability among them—appear to
be what people are seeking, before we can put them in order
and clarify them.

In any event, and quite apart from the desirability of having such a definition and classification now or later, I do believe
that this essay has demonstrated at least three things that are
of potential significance. And I believe it has done so because
of the Law and Economics approach it undertook. These are as
follows:

First, there are sets of goods and bads whose optimization
through pure market and pure command is counterproductive,
impossible even. These goods exist, however, and must be recognized and dealt with. Their quantity and quality in our society are the product of many modified market and modified
command decision systems that our society uses. We must
consider whether and to what degree these decision systems are
good, bad, or capable of improvement.

Second, the examination and incorporation of modified
markets and modified command systems into economic theory, if it could be done, would be immensely useful.[37]

Third, and almost in passing, goods—and not only odd
ones like altruism, but traditional, straightforward ones, like
caviar and potatoes—must be recognized as often being *both*
means and ends.[38] They are both what is wanted for their own
special attributes and what is wanted as a means of achieving
some other goals, such as satisfying our hunger or our need for
health care. And, again just in passing, this dual characteristic of
many goods helps us to understand real-world phenomena far
beyond altruism. When incorporated into economic theory, it
also helps us better to understand other aspects of economic reality, such as, for example, the relationship between economically

superior and inferior goods. The reason that, if we are poorer, we spend more on some goods, and drive their price up, in contrast to what happens as to other goods, is directly related—I believe—to the attribute that many goods have of being both means and ends. More dramatically, this dual attribute may even help us understand phenomena like the difference between Martin Luther King, Jr., and Malcolm X as to the desirability of violent versus nonviolent means to achieve change, or of the market as against command as ways of getting to a desired result. Each can be examined with respect to its *effectiveness* in bringing change about. But each is also desired as a good—or despised as a bad—in and of itself.[39]

VI

Of the Relationship of Markets and Command in the Liability Rule

A.

Since Douglas Melamed and I wrote about the liability rule some forty-five years ago,[1] it has been commonplace to view the rule as central to law, especially in fields like torts and eminent domain.[2] Rather than having transfers of entitlements come about either (a) as a result of market negotiations between the holder of the entitlement and the person or activity that seeks or needs it or (b) as a result of direct command decisions, a liability rule regime permits the person who wishes or needs to take the entitlement to get it by paying a collectively set price, even if the holder of the entitlement does not consent to the exchange.[3] Such a regime is, hence, a paradigmatic mixture of command and market approaches. Indeed, in another early article, I called the liability rule "the paradigmatic law of the mixed society," and asserted that it will be most widely used in those societies—namely, social democratic societies—in which the reigning ideology is neither libertarian nor collectivist.[4]

In the last forty-five years, the relation between the liability rule and rules of negotiation and command has been the subject of a huge literature. Our article, commonly referred to as "The Cathedral," has reportedly become the most cited private law article ever.[5] Not only has the literature that has grown out of "The Cathedral" been vast;[6] it has also made many important contributions. And yet there is something problematic about much of that literature, something I focused on recently in my article titled "A Broader View of the Cathedral."[7] That problem bears directly on the theme of this book and, hence, is worth discussing here as well.

In most of the literature on the liability rule and perhaps, albeit unconsciously, in Melamed's and my original article itself, there is a seeming assumption that the collectively set price, on the basis of which compelled shifts in entitlements will be allowed to take place, should mimic or approach the negotiated price that would obtain in a free market. The very use of the term "price" rather than "penalty" or "assessment" to describe the collectively set amount that must be paid to shift entitlements reflects the same market-mimicking underlying assumption.[8]

But that assumption—and here is where the theme of the present book becomes directly relevant—is simply not an accurate reflection of how the liability rule is *actually* employed in the legal world. As we shall soon see, while there certainly are times when the liability rule is used to approach what a free market would do were such a market feasible, there are many occasions when use of the liability rule reflects very different aims. Of course, the liability rule is not infrequently used when large number problems and high transaction costs make free-market negotiations difficult—in which case, the price collectively set often *is* designed to approach the outcome to which a free negotiation would have led. But even a quick look at the *actual* operation of the liability rule in tort and eminent domain law reveals both frequent applications of the rule that are very different and, not surprisingly, a setting of the price that is *not at all* designed to mirror what the market would establish.

It is to these real life examples that I now turn. I will later reflect, briefly, on what these examples tell us about the relationship between markets and command generally.

B.[9]

Let us look then at the actual use of liability rules in torts and its cognates. There are instances when the collectively set price seems to be designed to mirror the market, but there are also instances when use of a liability rule appears to further collective allocation decisions as well as instances when, instead, it can best be explained by a desire to achieve more nuanced social-democratic goals.

Let us start with torts—I shall discuss the more dramatic eminent domain examples in a bit. What is going on when a legal system allows punitive damages or gives juries free rein to set compensatory damages at levels that are far greater than those that would make the victim whole? At times, such punitive damages do mimic the market. This market-mimicking function is implicit in discussions of the multiplier effect by Sharkey and by Polinsky and Shavell, as well as in opinions by Judge Posner and by me that suggest the multiplier's efficiency.[10] Punitive damages perform the same function when they are given to reflect an extra value that a particular person places on a good because that person would not consent to give up that good in a free market at the good's ordinary market price. That is why I find Viscusi's discussion of punitive damages and lost airplane luggage to be inadequate.[11] I do not dispute that such luggage may well not be worth the protection that Viscusi's survey participants sought to give to it. But to assume that it is not is to overlook the extra "private value" that people often place on possessions of theirs that are not for sale. In such cases, punitive damages may be set to approximate the price that would be paid if a so-called property rule protected those possessions.

But there are other times when punitive damages and runaway-jury "compensatory" damages cannot be explained in this manner. In such cases, another explanation can be readily seen. The collectivity does not *want* the entitlement to be easily shifted. For any number of reasons, the collectivity may be reluctant to make the taking of the entitlement a penal matter, but may still want to deter its occurrence. That is, the collectivity may not wish to let the entitlement shift hands simply because the would-be taker is willing to pay a market price, even a market price with an appropriate multiplier. By assessing very high damages, and making these part of the liability rule, the collectivity seeks to make the entitlement come close to *inalienability*.[12]

Conversely, there are areas of tort law in which the damages assessed are self-consciously less than their market value. Obvious examples include the denial of so-called fanciful damages and the strict limitations on granting either purely emotional or purely economic damages.[13] Again, such rules can at times find market-mimicking cost-reduction explanations. The sufferer of fanciful damages may be the cheapest cost avoider.[14] Purely emotional injuries may, if compensated, increase in size; that is, people may feel emotional harm more if they are given the right to recover for it.[15] And solely economic damages may be best handled directly through contracts. Yet these explanations—worthy though they are, in my view—have never seemed completely satisfactory.

I would suggest that another set of reasons may at times be at work. These may be areas in which the collectivity wishes—for whatever reasons of its own—to make it easier than it otherwise would be in a purely consensual market to shift entitlements as well as to engage in activities that result in entitlement shifts.[16] Just as large extra-compensatory damages may reflect a collective decision to approach inalienability, so too systematically undercompensating damages may be the result of a collective decision to encourage those acts or activities that result in entitlement changes! The failure to give multiplier damages (or, for that matter, to permit class actions as a way of recognizing multiplier effects)[17] may also represent a decision of precisely this sort.

When one realizes that the liability rule is not merely used to do what a market is unable to do but, instead, acts as an independent instrument of collective decision making, its seemingly peculiar application in these areas becomes readily explainable. Whether the size of damages is designed to approach inalienability or to make shifts in entitlements relatively easier or harder than would occur in a purely consensual market, the explanation for the price chosen lies in a collective decision with respect to what entitlement shifts are relatively desirable as well as with respect to when they are desirable and when they are not.

Let me be clear, though. I am not saying that such decisions are necessarily wise or good. That is a different matter; they may or may not be. What I am saying is that, when one looks at the world of torts and tort damages *as it actually is,* one sees significant—occasionally dramatic—instances of liability rules being used not only to mimic the market but also to approach criminal or regulatory law results, as well as to bring about shifts in entitlements, and in levels of activities that cause entitlements changes, that are *different* from those that would occur either in a full market or in a full command structure. Once one recognizes the existence of these varied uses of the liability rule, one is much better placed to analyze and discuss whether the collectively set price and the goals that the collectivity had in mind in setting that price are good, bad, or indifferent. In other words, one is able to examine and criticize social-democratic goals *on their own terms* and not just in how well they achieve purely libertarian or purely collectivist aims.

The multiplicity of uses of the liability rule that one can see already in torts is even more obvious and dramatic in the law of eminent domain and takings, that other great employer of the liability rule. There are, of course, situations in which a taking is not permitted and a change in entitlements can only occur consensually. There are others in which a taking is banned and a consensual exchange is also forbidden.[18] But takings law concerns itself primarily with contexts in which a taking is allowed *and* a collectively set price is assessed on the taker. That is, much of takings law is liability-rule law. But what is the price to be assessed?

We commonly assume that the price must be that which would obtain in an unforced sale, in other words, the free-market price. That is, we commonly assume that takings law is designed to mimic the market. But that is not, in fact, always the case or always what is desired. In Italy (and I believe at one time in many other countries as well), when property was taken for a public purpose, the compensation paid was not the market value of the property, but its value in use.[19] If the owner of a large estate preferred to keep the property in a luxury or farming use, even though selling it for development would yield a far higher price, the owner was free to do so. But if the state decided to expropriate the property for a public purpose, then the owner was stuck with the use which he or she had chosen and would receive no more than the value of the property in that use.

I have some personal experience with such expropriation, at least according to family legend. It is said that my great uncle's lands outside Bologna had significant value. He had, however, opted not to develop the lands or to sell them for development. Whether he did so because, as an economist, he had figured that the lands' development value would increase faster than the interest rate he would receive on an earlier sale's gains, or because he enjoyed being a landowner, does not matter. He kept the lands in farming use. When the polity decided to build an airport near Bologna and saw that the large undeveloped lands belonging to my uncle were well situated for an airport, they took his lands by eminent domain. They paid him only the lands' rather meager farming value, making him—and me, I suppose—much less well off than we would have been had they been required to pay the market value of the property.

Why might such a nonmarket compensation price be set? My uncle, good economist that he was, always described this situation as one of the many instances in which the law failed to understand economics. And, in his case, that may even have been true. But it is also conceivable that a polity might wish to encourage entitlement shifts from passive landowners to more aggressive uses, including public-purpose ones. By setting the liability-rule price at the value-in-use level, the polity tells landowners that they retain their "lordly" use at a peril (should the polity desire the property for a public purpose). And this price-setting decision also furthers a private, consensual, market-value change in entitlements, with the landowner acting out of fear of being subjected to the lower public-purpose price, should a public-purpose taking later come to be desired. Again, it is not for me here to discuss the pros and cons of such an approach. It is sufficient for my purposes that the social-democratic decision to devalue "lordly" uses of entitlements relative to other uses is readily apparent in the decision not to compensate takings at the market value of the property.

Significantly, there are also times when a polity's collective values seem to justify pricing private property at *more* than its market value for takings purposes. Recently, private homes in New London, Connecticut, were expropriated to further a re-development scheme.[20] The public purpose was the commercial improvement and upgrading of the area (and perhaps even its gentrification) for the benefit of the city. But the immediate beneficiaries of the right to take the property by eminent domain were private developers. The homeowners objected strenuously to the taking of their properties. Ultimately, however, the U.S. Supreme Court upheld that taking.[21] The result was considerable anger and even demonstrations at the home of Justice Souter, who had joined the Court's majority opinion.[22]

Interestingly, during oral argument, Justice Kennedy asked whether eminent domain would not be much more acceptable if, in such circumstances, although the taking for a public purpose would still be allowed, the price to be paid were some multiple of—say, four times—the market price.[23] What he was suggesting, it seems to me, was that, while nonconsensual entitlement shifts might still be properly permitted in situations like the one in *Kelo,* the change in entitlements might—for good collective reasons—nonetheless be discouraged through the setting of a higher liability-rule price. In other words, the polity could appropriately take a view of the ease with which such entitlement changes should occur that is the opposite of the view taken by Bologna with respect to my uncle's lands. Both Justice Kennedy's suggestion in *Kelo* and the value-in-use approach are examples of a liability rule being employed to further *collective* aims, while still not going to a fully command entitlement structure.[24]

The same would be as true for a polity that assessed larger than compensatory tort damages when environmentally desirable uses were infringed upon,[25] as for a polity that, conversely, limited such damages in order to further industrialization. And if this fact, inevitably, makes torts scholars think of the development of negligence as a general requirement for liability in the nineteenth century, together with the continued applicability of nonfault liability in England when industry infringed on traditional, "natural" uses of land (as in *Rylands v. Fletcher*),[26] I would just add that it only shows that the nuanced, middle use of liability rules that I am describing is nothing new. One hundred fifty years ago, as today, the liability rule was no mere mimicker of the market or of full collective aims; rather, it was then, and continues to be now, the instrument of goals that reflect both collectivist and libertarian choice elements.[27]

C.

But this is not all that a real-world look at the categories described in "The Cathedral" article tells us. That article also described shifts in entitlements that were excluded from the market or from liability rule–based exchanges. These command-determined entitlement shifts were called inalienability rules. Yet, early on, in what is still as good an article as anyone has written about "The Cathedral" and is, in my terminology, a paradigmatic example of Law and Economics scholarship, Susan Rose-Ackerman wrote that what "The Cathedral" called inalienability was, in fact, many different rules.[28] Entitlements might be, for example, given, but not sold; sold, but not destroyed; destroyed, but neither sold nor transferred by gift; and so forth. In that early article, Rose-Ackerman, in effect, pointed out that what "The Cathedral" had assumed to be a pure and simple command regime was immensely nuanced and much more complicated. By looking at the actual world, she was doing to inalienability what here, and in "A Broader View of the Cathedral," I am currently doing with respect to the liability rule.[29]

She there asserted, as I do now, that in the world of law the relationship between markets and command is extraordinarily complex. The canonical but inadequate view of the liability rule may have treated that rule as being a modified market. However, not only modified markets and modified command structures exist; the two, in fact, meld into each other, such that clear lines as to which approach dominates may be very hard to draw in a given instance.

Why is it difficult to distinguish these different uses of the liability rule? There are, I think, at least two reasons, both of which bring us back to comments and analyses that Coase proffered in "The Nature of the Firm."[30] First, as Coase noted in that still amazingly seminal article, the command structures represented by firms might be employed not only where, and because, they were cheaper than markets, but also because people *liked* command structures. In other words, Coase saw already back then what I noted earlier in my discussion of altruism—namely, that there are goods that are both ends and means.[31] And, interestingly, Coase (in his Socialist youth) saw *command structures* as such a good. It is not hard to see in the writings of many great libertarians an equivalent view of *markets*.[32]

Arguments can and should be made with respect to the use of command structures and market structures based on their relative efficiency as means, that is, based on their relative capacity to get us *results*. But such an analysis is incomplete, for it leaves out why some would want to use a market or a command structure even when it is less efficient, more costly, than some alternative. It fails to consider that some people *like* markets, while others *like* command, and that this preference is in their utility functions. As Coase saw, and mentioned in passing, we may not be able fully to explain the existence of firms without understanding that fact. Earlier in this book, I said the same thing with respect to the persistence of not-for-profit institutions. What needs to be added here is that the same holds for the wide-ranging use of *mixed* command and market structures and, specifically and importantly, for the use of the liability rule in all of its *varied* forms.

The liability rule is used to approach what a market would do but can't, efficiently. It is also used to approach what direct collective allocations would do but can't, efficiently. The liability rule may also be used, however, because it is an approach that a social democratic polity *likes,* in and of itself. And where the polity's preference for this approach is partly the reason for its use, it should not be surprising that the amount charged to permit entitlement changes might mirror neither the *price* that a market would set nor the *penalty* that a pure command structure would impose. In such instances, the *assessment* that both allows and limits entitlement shifts may be chosen to reflect that polity's liking for, and devotion to, its ideologically mixed foundation.

I have, of course, used the terms "price," "penalty," and "assessment," above, intentionally to indicate when the liability rule is being used, respectively, in place of a market, in place of a command, and for reasons having to do with its own ideological desirability. But I must confess that, in many instances, I cannot say which of the three is represented by the charge made under the liability rule. It is often difficult to say, not only because the effect of ideological desires for libertarianism, collectivism, or social democracy may be hard to weigh in particular situations, but also because the use of markets, commands, and hybrids of the two, like liability rules, may stem from their cost-effectiveness rather than from their inherent desirability. It is to this aspect—the cost-effectiveness of the different approaches—that I now briefly turn.

When Coase noted, again in passing, that firms—the command structures he was describing as dominating—were not centralized command structures but private, decentralized ones, he was indicating that mixed approaches—modified markets and modified commands—are often more cost-effective than pure approaches. That insight has been restated and applied by others since.[33] Just as the complex mixed use of modified markets and modified commands bore examining in the contexts of merit goods and of altruism, so too it deserves mention in the liability-rule context. Apart from the inherent desirability of markets, commands, and hybrids in different situations—in other words, apart from the fact that we may *like* each of these approaches in different contexts—why do liability-rule charges sometimes look like prices, sometimes like penalties, and sometimes like assessments? The explanation may be, in part, due to the fact that liability rules—not as ends in themselves, but as means to other ends—are, in different situations, most cost-effective by approximating prices, penalties, or assessments.

The reason that liability-rule charges often look like, and are properly described as, prices has been much discussed in the "Cathedral" literature. When liability rules are more efficient than consensual exchanges has been thoroughly examined, both in relatively simple and in highly complex empirical contexts, and warrants no further discussion here.[34] Far less attention has been paid, however, to when the liability rule is used as a civil penalty because it achieves inalienability or command-like results more effectively than command or administrative law would. This essay is not the place to go deeply into the question. But a few words, which may lead others to research the issue more thoroughly, may be appropriate.

The most obvious case is where a liability rule is used as a penalty because individual enforcement by those who receive the penalty is thought to be more likely than state enforcement. Treble damages in RICO and antitrust law may well be instances of this. Direct government command, through criminal or administrative sanctions, is available. But the liability rule— at a penalty level—is also there, at least in part so that deterrence approaching prohibition will occur even when the government does not deem it worthwhile to act.[35] There are other more nuanced situations as well, though. For various moral or even religious reasons, a polity may not want to make certain conduct criminal, and yet may wish to deter it nearly totally. A huge liability-rule assessment approaching in force a criminal sanction may then be optimal. One rather dramatic example, so ably discussed by Shmueli, is the use of the liability rule to induce orthodox Jewish males to issue a "get" and thereby allow their wives a religious divorce and remarriage.[36]

There are many other situations, of course, and if one puts together the insight in Susan Rose-Ackerman's classic article on how complex inalienability really is,[37] with how varied the "price," "assessment," or "penalty" that a liability rule imposes can be, one sees that much work remains to be done even here where so much has already been written.

VII
Of Tastes and Values Ignored

There are two distinct parts to my views on how economics treats, and should treat, tastes and values. The first concerns those tastes, values, and costs that many economists seem to ignore, or treat as irrational or not worth paying attention to. They do this while at the same time taking the position that, as to the validity and merit of tastes and values, economics has nothing to say. In this essay I will first examine the nature of this paradoxical—inconsistent even—attitude. Then I will explain some potentially sound reasons for what economic theory is in fact doing when it accepts some tastes, values, and costs, and rejects others. And I will conclude with a plea for more openness and clarity in the treatment of such tastes, values, and costs.[1]

The next essay, instead, will argue that economists are very well suited—perhaps are optimally suited—to examine the consequences of some tastes and values. I will assert that with a minimum of assumptions of a sort that are standard in economic theory, economists can give lawmakers guidance in favoring laws that further the creation of some values and deter others. I will then argue that with very few changes, of a sort that are consonant with the structure of economics, economic theory can become a powerful tool in the reform, criticism, and confirmation of what, *in fact*, is one of the law's most important functions, the furtherance of some values and the deterrence of others.

A.

The attitude of many economists toward values, tastes, and—what in many instances is simply the other side of the same coin—whether costs are real, seems to me to be profoundly inconsistent. On the one hand, it is standard economic rubric to say that, as to tastes and values, economists have nothing to say. Whether people want or like caviar or bananas is their business, and all economics can do is start from a given set of tastes and values and then analyze the consequences of these wants, however meritorious or noxious a noneconomist might deem them. *De gustibus non est disputandum*—as to tastes there is no sense arguing—is almost a creed in economics. And if tastes and values are taken as a given, so too are the costs—the effect of distastes—that tastes and values entail. I like silence; therefore, my neighbor's taste for—and desire to make—noise is costly to me. As to both, classic economics says, this field has nothing to say.

But despite this fundamental assertion, I believe it is demonstrable that economists, in their work, take positions with respect to the relative merits of different tastes, values, and resulting costs, and do so all the time. Not infrequently there are plausible reasons for economists' choices in this respect, reasons rooted in what economists believe they can handle in the models they make and use. At other times, however, the devaluing of some tastes and values is hard to understand. But apart from that, in all instances where such depreciation of some categories of tastes and values occurs, more self-consciousness and explicit recognition of what is going on would not merely be helpful; such recognition is in fact essential if economics is to be used to examine law and legal structures. It may be undesirable, or even impossible, for economics to take into account some tastes, values, and resulting costs. But the fact that these are ignored or degraded surely affects the usefulness of any economic analysis of law and of legal structures. To the extent that these legal structures derive from, or have been created in reaction to, ignored costs and values, the worthiness of those costs and values has to be considered.

Let me give some examples. I will begin by discussing some costs and values whose setting aside seems to me to be completely unjustified. I will then focus on more difficult ones—ones, incidentally, already adverted to and used in my earlier analysis of altruism and of merit goods.

A distinguished lawyer-economist, Kip Viscusi, wrote an article a few years ago in which he asserted that giving punitive damages to the owners of luggage lost by airlines was senseless.[2] The losers should be reimbursed only the "cost" of their luggage. Airfares, Viscusi argued, would rise significantly if punitive damages were awarded, and to no good purpose.

To no good purpose? That conclusion may well be correct, but it depends entirely on whether the owners of the lost luggage may properly demand that their luggage be—to use the terms that Melamed and I first used in our "Cathedral" article[3]—protected by a property rather than a liability rule. If they may do so, then paying them the collectively determined price of their luggage, rather than a premium represented by punitive damages, undercompensates them for their loss. To say that they should not receive that greater compensation, in effect, is to say that the luggage owners have no right to value their luggage, or the harm to them of having an airline lose it, more highly than the collectively determined liability rule eminent domain price.

Were the damage not to luggage, but to kidneys or to private parts, it would seem odd to say that it was senseless for an individual to give a special value, one not recognized in the market, to his or her body. But why may not individuals, for whatever reasons, value their suitcases and abhor the loss of them by airlines in a way different from what the collectivity would judge the suitcase and its content to be worth in the market? It is not a valid objection to this to say that so valuing them is uncertain, difficult, or expensive. In principle, that these individuals prefer to have values that are costly should be of no more concern to the economist than that some individuals prefer caviar to bananas, and surely to potatoes. If de gustibus non est disputandum is the rule, why should we call senseless people who have a special luggage-affection? It's their taste.

Now it may be that what Viscusi is saying is something quite different. He may, for instance, be saying that it is difficult to make luggage-lovers bear the costs (in higher fares) of luggage-loving. And, for that reason, he may be saying that a legal structure that raises the airfares to many who would prefer lower fares and lower compensation is bad. And he may well be right, but with the caveat that any such assertion implies a distributional judgment among luggage-lovers and luggage-care-nots. What he cannot say, or even imply, however, is that those who want punitive damages are irrational. Indeed, few things are more rational than seeking something that one does not have to pay for in full! And it cannot, therefore, be said that a system of luggage-loss punitive damages is senseless. Whether, in actuality, punitive damages are good or bad requires a specific consideration of the merits of one set of tastes as against another, and also of the distributional consequences of the alternate legal structures for luggage-lovers versus luggage-care-nots.[4]

In the end, unless supported by extremely complicated distributional and other analyses, the assertion by Viscusi—like the now long-since Coase-destroyed Pigouvian assertions as to who should necessarily bear the cost of noise or pollution— seems rather to reflect an implicit belief that loving luggage is silly and should not be given weight. In other words, it constitutes a view that this particular taste should, for the benefit of society, be ignored. That may well be right, but it is a statement as to what values are worth having and what are not. From an *economics* point of view, it is the equivalent of saying that a taste for caviar is something that somehow society should discourage people from having.

Viscusi's treatment of the value some give to their luggage is easily described as an example of implicit valuation and rejection of some tastes. More interesting, but ultimately no different, would be if the Viscusian criticism were directed at the value individuals give to their luggage only when that luggage *is lost by an airline.* That is, can economists properly say, you have a right to give some extra value to your luggage, to love it, so to speak, but you do not have a right to give it that extra value, and treat its loss as more costly than usual, when it is lost by an airline?

I think not, if de gustibus non est disputandum is to be the rule. I may value caviar more at breakfast than I do at tea, and charge those who would deprive me of my breakfast snack with causing me more pain than would result if they imposed only a tea-caviar prohibition. And so it must be with respect to airline luggage losses versus, say, home misplacements.

Indeed, as Viscusi himself has so ably pointed out, people do regularly give values to things, and especially to their lives, in context.[5] Losing one's life in some ways is—for whatever reasons—deemed much more costly than losing it in other ways. The fear of terrorism and the costs undertaken to block terrorists is but one of the most dramatic and recent examples of such differences in valuation. As lawmakers, we may deem such attitudes desirable, or not. But as economists who purport to be agnostic as to tastes, we have no more right to describe such context-related values as irrational or bad than we have to judge the merits of a taste for broccoli, in general, or for eating broccoli only at the seashore.

B.

The type of taste/value assumptions by economists just described are easily criticized. There are others, however, that are common in economics and whose reasons for being are more defensible. But I believe that the way economics often approaches the existence even of these leaves a lot to be desired.

1.

As I mentioned in earlier essays, economists have sometimes ignored the desire for altruism and beneficence that *in fact* many people have, and other economists have tended to downplay the objection that, for whatever reasons, many people have to the allocation of certain goods on the basis of the prevailing wealth distribution. Similarly, at times, no heed is paid to the objections made to the too obvious pricing—to the commodification—of some goods. Conversely, some seem to ignore the objections made to too obvious allocation by the state of goods and bads—what I have called commandification. Structures set up to attenuate the wealth dependency of the first set of goods are, for instance, not infrequently described as Pareto inferior, even though that can only be said if the costs/harms to the objectors are ignored. Moreover, and more generally, as I've noted in my article "The Pointlessness of Pareto," there are costs whose existence makes impossible reorganizations which, if they occurred, would make all people better off.[6] These costs are regularly treated by economists as nonexistent. And the reorganizations that do not, in fact, occur because of these costs are typically described as necessarily desirable moves to the Pareto frontier.

Why are all these costs and values so frequently ignored? Let me treat each of them separately, and then after generalizing from these separate discussions, make some suggestions for a more useful handling of such costs and values.

I have earlier indicated that the reason that the value that people place on the existence of altruistic and beneficent behavior, both in its individual and in its governmental forms, is that it is hard to handle a good that cannot be successfully optimized by pure market or pure command structures. And I still think that is a fair statement. The fact that it is equally meaningless to ask, How much must I pay you to love me for myself alone? and How can I command you to love me for myself alone? remains a succinct way of explaining what is troubling in this area. But I think more needs to be said.

The value that people give to the existence of beneficent behavior is—for the above-mentioned reason—not manifested in the market in the same way that the value that people give to caviar is. We can see the relative price of caviar—in its various

Beluga and Sevruga forms, in relation to other fish roes, and in comparison to other foodstuffs—quite directly. It is, therefore, quite easy to say, People have a taste for it, value it, despite its expensiveness. That is much harder to do with respect to beneficence and altruism. Of course—as many economists have done—we can look at the existence of altruistic behavior or structures as ways of getting from A to C. And we can examine whether they are more expensive than self-interested behavior or structures would be as ways of going the same distance; of getting to the same result. Conversely, we can—as I suggested earlier—look at the payments given to CEOs of not-for-profits. And from these we can infer that people are, in fact, willing to pay very highly for the sake of satisfying their desire for beneficence. But that is still not the kind of data furnished by the price of caviar in the market.

In other words, it is nowhere near as easy to introduce the cost/value data that characterize our view of altruistic behavior and structures into models as it is for ordinary goods through ordinary pricing data. And the problem is exacerbated by the fact that most of the time even such direct-money data as might exist with respect to altruism are not in fact available. Do we actually know the different costs that a for-profit and a not-for-profit bear in achieving a similar goal, like the delivery of health care? What we have, instead, is the use of any number of mixed, semi-, hemi-, demi- market incentives designed to increase the amount of altruism or to channel it into areas that seem best. Use of *some* semimarket means designed to satisfy our altruistic longings—to the greatest extent at the least cost—can, I think, be documented. But the conversion of these into figures that lend themselves to modeling, to economic analysis in what has become the canonical way of doing that analysis, is very hard.[7]

When economics was less model dependent, less mathematical, more political economy than econometrics, the difficulty of converting such cost/value/price data surrounding altruism in its various manifestations into the kind of data that the caviar market readily provides might not have mattered that much. Why, then, not simply return to that sort of "political economy?" Even to ask this question is, however, to ignore why economics has become what it is today. The type of analysis that characterizes much of current economics has become dominant because it has let economics, in distinct contrast to other social sciences, be more rigorous, more scientific and, as a result, more logically powerful in the conclusions it reaches. Other social sciences have, to greater or lesser extents, tried to emulate economics in this.[8] But because they have been able to handle less of what is of core interest to them in this way than has economics, they have been less successful than economics in making such a move. Economics *can* be mathematical, model based—and within its own terms highly rigorous—and still deal with much that is its "meat and potatoes." Little wonder that it has increasingly become what it is!

Under the circumstances, the reluctance to take head-on the challenge that altruism poses, when it is viewed as a value, as something people want and are willing to pay a lot for, albeit not in simplistic ordinary prices, is more than understandable. This is not to say that some—often great—economists have not considered the problem, though perhaps in an older, but still attractive, political economy way.[9] And the lawyer-economist cannot help but admire these and ask, If economists such as these do not take that challenge on, who will? The same lawyer-economist is also tempted to ask, Is it so clear that, perhaps with simplifying assumptions, the cost/pricing that surrounds altruism in its various forms cannot be incorporated into highly sophisticated economic models of the modern sort? All too often scholars ignore what is hard. Great scholars take it on and find ways of resolving the difficulties, or at least of reducing them sufficiently so as to deal adequately with the hardest of problems.

To the lawyer-economist who looks at existing legal structures, the lack of a complex, modeled economic analysis that takes full account of the desire people have for altruism and its effect on the market and on the resulting panoply of legal structures presents a major problem. That is why *this* lawyer-economist, who has great faith in the ability of economists, asks economists to take on the challenge of integrating the costs and pricings that surround altruism *as an end* into economic theory and models. It may not be as easy as was—after Coase—the integration into economic models of the fact that markets are, in fact, costly. But, in the end, it may be feasible and, if it were, it would surely be as fruitful.

Similarly, though perhaps easier, would be the integration into standard economic analysis of the fact that in this area *modified* command structures are commonly employed. Discussion of command, as an alternative to markets, readily permits the consideration of varied types of command structures and their relative costs and benefits. A recognition that command does not necessarily, or even often, entail centralized, clear, governmental decisions is something that has to be part of any contrast between the market—in its differing forms—and its costs, and the various command alternatives and their costs. Again, once one accepts, with Coase, that firms exist because in some situations the command structure that firms exemplify is more efficient than the market, one cannot help asking, But why did *this* command structure establish itself rather than any number of other possible command structures? Not surprisingly, much excellent work of precisely this sort has, in fact, been done by distinguished economists.[10]

I believe that an analysis of the various forms of command that are available is essential to an understanding of how the demand for altruism and beneficence is met in our society, and to gauging whether it is well or badly met. As is the case with respect to any analysis of the modified markets that are used to "optimize" altruism, making such an analysis of different command situations *as applied to altruism,* and—this is the rub—*integrated with the use of modified markets in this area,* is not easy. But once again, I believe that at least part of that analysis is best made by economists, and so challenge them to try to do it.

Unlike the integration of the existence of suitcase lovers into economic analysis (which can readily be done), what is required of economics, if altruism is to be treated in a way that is both true to the reality of people's desires and useful to those who must gauge legal structures, may not be feasible. And I will, later in this essay, make some suggestions as to what should be done if it is not. But I hope, and rather think, economic theory is, in fact, up to handling the matter.

2.

Failing to give weight to the costs and values that lie behind the existence of merit goods is in some ways easier and in some ways harder to understand than the equivalent failure with respect to the desire for altruism/beneficence. What seems to be involved here is a reluctance to take into account the effects on an individual's utility of decisions made by other individuals, when these effects do not have intervening material consequences, when, in other words, the utility costs are moral.

Another person's actions in a market transaction that cause harm to those not directly involved in that transaction are classically dealt with in economics. They are the source of precisely those externalities that, since Coase we know, individuals seek to minimize through their own market actions. Moreover, both before and after Coase, we have seen that these are often the object of collective interventions designed either to internalize them (to make them part of the market transactions which caused them), or to reduce them directly. (Which among these ways of reacting to such externalities predominates—as, since Coase, we all know—depends on the relative size of both the transaction costs and the collective-action costs that the different remedies would impose, and on our inherent liking of—our utility preference for—market and collective actions.)

Why should the external costs that attach to merit goods be any less real or any less properly subject to economic consideration and analysis? Well, they are moral costs rather than direct material costs. But that would hardly seem to matter. Moral costs are simply a statement of what I value. I am just as likely to pay you to move out of town, to the next village, because I don't like you and don't want you near me, as I am to pay you to move out of town because, for purely financial reasons, I prefer that you build a gazebo in the next village rather than next door to me. To the economist, it should not matter. What lie behind merit goods are *external* moral costs rather than *direct* moral costs like those recognized in the above-mentioned transaction. But again, why should this matter?

Indeed, it generally doesn't. Economics has no problem taking into account the "external" cost to me of your buying a house next door to me, when your being there offends me because you make noise, indulge in sex without drawing your shades, or are abhorrent to me because of your religion, race, gender, or sexual orientation. The law and the lawyer may say that some of these moral externalities are to be given weight, that others are to be ignored, and that even the cognizance of still others *must* be prohibited. And this the law does with respect to material externalities as well. Thus, law may give weight to, ignore, or prohibit consideration of the fact that when you buy a house next door, your presence there increases or diminishes the value of my house. All these law-reactions are collective actions taken with respect to these externalities. And, as such, they may be good or bad.

But the economist, if truly wedded to the notion that de gustibus non est disputandum, cannot speak *a priori* to whether these external moral costs are proper or not. The economist cannot choose to treat them as improper or nonexistent and on that basis to decry the actions taken by the collectivity in response to them. To the extent people suffer from bearing external moral costs and wish to minimize them, there would seem to be no reason why the collective responses that result should be any more questioned than *any* collective responses to *any* external costs.

Why, then, do some economists state that actions taken by the collectivity to remove some goods and bads from the ordinary markets and to allocate them in less wealth distribution–dependent ways must be described as Pareto inferior?[11] The question is especially pressing because no one suggests that individual, altruistic payments to cause individuals to act differently in their purchase and sale of such merit goods violate the Pareto norm. If private, market-like expenditures, designed to modify the actions of the buyers and sellers of merit goods, and thereby to reduce the external moral costs these create, present no Pareto problems, why should collective actions do so? Which approach, market or collective, predominates, any Coasean should say, is likely to depend on the relative cost-effectiveness of private-versus-collective action (as well as which we inherently *like*). The actual treatment of merit goods that prevails in the world that the lawyer sees seems to be one in which some privately paid for modifications of the behavior of the buyers and sellers of merit goods can be identified, but in which many more modifications are brought about through collective intervention.[12]

As to all of these, an argument may be made that a different mix of collective and private internalizations would work better. (I will treat, soon enough, the question of how one should deal with the *costs* that *making* such an argument entails. These costs, which are the costs of convincing people that what they are doing is Pareto inferior, or at least Kaldor-Hicks inferior, present a problem all their own.)[13] But what seems to me to be *prima facie* not acceptable is for an economist—who asserts that the values and desires that people have is none of his or her business as an economist—to act as though the external morals costs that define merit goods are either nonexistent or are irrational and that they are, therefore, to be ignored without discussion or analysis. This is equally true, moreover, whether the external costs are those associated with anti-commodification/anti-commandification merit goods or with wealth distribution/power distribution–dependent merit goods. As to both, denying that powerful external moral costs, which shape behavior and hence the legal structure, exist is either willfully ignoring the reality of people's wants and values, or making an *a priori* judgment as to what values are good and what values are not!

Why, then, are such external moral costs so frequently set aside? Is it because, as with altruism, the ways of dealing with them too often involve modified markets and modified collective techniques? I think not. With respect to altruism, modified markets are needed to determine the desire for altruism—the value given to altruism by individuals. And that creates problems of quantification and modeling. As to merit goods, modified markets and modified command are used to allocate these goods because their allocation through the ordinary market causes significant external moral costs. The recognition of these moral costs, which is the issue before us, does not at all, however, depend on modified markets. How one values moral costs is always a problem. How one values moral costs that arise externally to a transaction—like the cost to me of your sale of your house, which is next to mine, to someone whose behavior I find despicable and offensive—is especially a problem. Whether the society should, or even constitutionally can, give weight to such costs is frequently an issue. (The external moral costs to a homeowner that arise from the sale of a neighboring house to someone whose race or religion the homeowner despises have long been constitutionally excluded from consideration.)[14] But whether to give these costs weight or not is an issue as to which, classically, the economist *qua* economist can take no stand, because it goes to values and tastes.

The external moral costs involved in merit goods are closely analogous. Some, like the external moral costs of campaign contributions based on wealth, may—rightly or wrongly— be constitutionally excluded from consideration.[15] Others, like the external moral costs of wartime military service based on wealth, have, at times, been the core reasons for the selective service systems that have been established.[16] Yet others, like those that attach to a wealth dependent market in body parts, seem to me to be largely responsible for the common prohibition of such a market as to many body parts.[17] The society's response to these costs clearly differs. But as to whether they *are* costs—to the economist *qua* economist—there should be no doubt. And if they are costs, then the suggestion that collective responses to them violate Pareto principles because they derogate from the transactions that gave rise to them cannot stand.

Why, then, do economists frequently seem to disvalue and ignore such costs? My best guess is that it is because the recognizing of these costs implicates recognition of something that creates great problems for economic modeling: the effect on one person's utility system of another person's utility reactions. Classic economic models do not take into account whether your happiness at buying bananas makes me sad or rejoice.[18] To take it into consideration makes things complicated. And in most cases, I would guess, such recognition is not significant enough to be worth the trouble of introducing it into the model. The game is not worth the candle. Hence, such simplifications are not only explainable, they are wise, if the discipline is to do relatively easily and well the tasks that it must do. To the degree, then, that recognition of the types of moral costs involved in merit good analysis implicates such interdependent utility considerations, one can understand why many economists are reluctant to recognize them.

But the consequences of the simplification, of the ignoring of these costs, *in this context* are totally different and of a different order from the consequences of paying no heed to interdependent utilities elsewhere. Here, legal structures that govern much of our lives can be explained only if such costs are recognized and what we should do about such costs is seriously examined. If economics declines, for its own reasons, to give them weight, then, by that very fact, economics removes itself from the discussion of the merits of the legal structures established in response to them. An Economic Analysis of Law that does not admit and include in its model these costs tells us little that is useful of the laws it analyzes in these areas!

Just as an economic model that denied that markets had costs was of little help in analyzing why, when, and what kinds of firms existed, so an economic model that gives no recognition to the external moral costs (a) of commodification and commandification of some goods, and (b) of the exchange, in a prevailing wealth distribution–dependent market, of other goods, is of little use in helping us to understand, criticize, and make better the legal structures that dominate fields as diverse as selective service, allocation of the right to have children, allocation of body parts, and even campaign contributions. Economics may have good reasons for insisting on this simplification. But the costs of such a simplification to the relevance of economics to crucial decisions cannot be ignored.

3.

My last example of an area in which economics seems—implicitly but commonly—to be taking a stand on which tastes and values (and the costs that result) should be considered and which ones, instead, should be treated as "not there," is rather different from those I have just been discussing. It deals with issues I treated in my article "The Pointlessness of Pareto."[19] In "The Pointlessness of Pareto," I argued that *we are always* at the Pareto frontier. If there really were a spot to which we could move that bettered some people and left none worse off, why wouldn't we already have gone there? And, I said, the fact that people don't realize or understand that such a Pareto-preferable position exists simply means that at the moment there are *knowledge costs* that keep us away from such a clearly preferable position. But, I added, outward moves *in* the Pareto frontier also result, precisely, from improved knowledge. It is always lack of knowledge that keeps us from bettering ourselves. What, then, I asked, is the difference between the knowledge costs that keep us from moving to the frontier, and those that keep the frontier from outward movements? In theory, there is no difference, and that is why I stated that we are always at the Pareto frontier.

My analysis depended, however, on the *recognition* of—on the giving weight to—those knowledge costs that are the reasons why we don't change things in ways that would, *ex post,* leave some better off, and none less well off. If such costs are properly to be treated differently from other costs, costs of, say, technological or organizational innovations, then Pareto can sleep undisturbed. If the knowledge costs of making available information that permits a move to what can be termed the frontier are not to be compared with the knowledge costs of achieving the technological changes that all would recognize as moves in the frontier, then classical Paretian analysis can remain untroubled.

And, not so incidentally, the analysis has similar implications for Kaldor-Hicks improvements.[20] These do not require the existence of "no losers"; they only require that gainers gain more than losers lose. As such, it is easy to see why losers, if able to do so, will block Kaldor-Hicks moves. The exact meaning of this for compensation and distribution analysis is not my current concern. My present point is to ask whether those who promote Kaldor-Hicks analyses, and make suggestions as to what changes should be made on the basis of such analyses, take into account the knowledge costs of that analysis and promotion. Do they, in saying that a given change creates more benefits than it costs, consider the costs both (a) of reaching that conclusion, and (b) of convincing individuals that such a

move would, indeed, be Kaldor-Hicks superior? Or do they, like
the *Paretians,* treat these knowledge costs as irrelevant to, and
not to be compared with, technological knowledge costs that
would allow totally different Kaldor-Hicks superior moves,
which could, so to speak, create new "Kaldor-Hicks frontiers"?

I would suggest that just as traditional economics has all
too often tended to ignore the fact that people value beneficence
as a good in itself, and the fact that people bear significant
moral costs when certain goods are allocated in ordinary market ways, so traditional economic theory has often ignored and
treated as nonexistent those knowledge costs that, in fact, prevent us from recognizing the existence of a point that, were we
there, would actually be Pareto superior, or at least Kaldor-Hicks
superior to our previous position. These costs are typically not
recognized and compared with other costs—of knowledge and
organization—that keep us from moving the frontier outward;
that keep us from being, all or in part, better off.

The reason these "moves-to-the-frontier" costs are not
treated like other costs is, I think, both obvious and understandable. That does not mean, however, that it is unproblematic. The
costs of moves to the frontier are the costs of doing what economists
do.[21] They are the costs of compensating them for their analyses
and for trying to convince others that these analyses are correct
and justify change. It may be that the costs of paying physicists to
do their job—the costs both of coming up with an innovation and
then of convincing others that the innovation they have come up
with is worth adopting—are less (or more), in relation to the
benefits achieved, than those that attach to paying economists.
And, at some level, the society will make just that comparison. But,
my iconoclastic view in "The Pointlessness of Pareto" to the contrary notwithstanding, it is easy to see why economists should not
introduce that comparison into their everyday analysis.

There are, in other words, great technical advantages in letting economists treat the costs of moving to the frontier as different in kind from other knowledge/technological costs. Doing so is what allows the discipline to define itself and to do the important work that it does. To that extent, *Paretian* and Kaldor-Hicks analyses are well worth doing. And we can, for such purposes, treat the costs of doing those analyses and of convincing others of their results as nonexistent. But to do that is, I would contend, different from denying their significance at a different level of analysis. In fact, such costs are as real and their size depends on values and tastes just as much as any other costs in society. It may well be that economics should pay these costs no heed most of the time. I rather think so. But what economists cannot properly do is to dismiss as irrational actions that are taken by people in the world at large that are based on the existence of such costs. In other words, when the issue is how much to allocate to, to spend on, economics and how much on physics, these costs are central and cannot be ignored. In this respect, the proper treatment of these costs, like the proper treatment of the costs and values that underlie the existence of altruism and of merit good costs, presents a challenge for economic theory. That challenge comes down to this: When is it appropriate to ignore costs and values in making an economic model, and when is it not?

C.

What can one say more generally about economics and the proper treatment of these troublesome types of costs and values? The first thing one can say is that "ignoring" or treating as "outside the model," let alone terming "irrational" or "unreal," any costs or tastes and values that people in fact have or bear, violates the assertion that economics has nothing to say about tastes or values. To ignore or treat as nonexistent some tastes and values—some things that are in individuals' utility functions, and the costs that result from their being there—constitutes a taking of a position—*sub silentio*—on tastes and values. And the fact that there may be good reasons for ignoring some values and costs no more alters this than does the fact that there are many values and tastes that people *do* decide all the time ought to be ignored or downgraded. To the extent that any taste or value is held by people, setting it aside involves a choice. And excluding it effectuates a ranking of values. This is so, moreover, even if the reason for setting such a taste or value aside stems not from a judgment of its validity, but from an incapacity to deal with that taste or value in one's model or one's discipline.

This does not mean that economics is unjustified in refusing to take into account some tastes, values, and their resulting costs. If an attempt to include in an economic model some values or tastes makes the modeling impossible, significantly less coherent, or just too difficult, and thereby renders the model less useful to the task for which the model was created, then exclusion of those tastes or values makes the best of sense. So, in appropriate circumstances, economists may be quite correct in refusing to take into account utility interdependencies. But this is not because such interdependencies don't exist; it is because including them in the model is too hard, and excluding them does not diminish the validity of the model's results significantly. As I've said earlier, the game is not worth the candle. The same justifies, in all sorts of situations, the unwillingness of economists to give weight to the very real information costs (both of analysis and of persuasion) that keep us from making moves to what, but for these costs, would be a

Pareto-superior position. Accordingly, blanket criticism of economics for making such exclusions is not correct.

This, however, does not mean that exclusions of this sort are not costly. How costly they are depends on the question that is being asked; the issue that is being analyzed. Accordingly, such exclusions may or may not make sense. As I've just noted, if the issue is how much a society should spend on economic science, as against physics, then the relative costs of moving to what (but for their existence) would be a Pareto-superior position, in comparison to the costs of making a physics discovery that would move the frontier outward, *is* the question. And acting as if "to the frontier" costs are nonexistent renders the discussion meaningless. Moreover, since *even the comparison between paying economists or physicists* may well be best made by economists, to say that economics can, as a general matter, ignore such costs is wrong.

The same applies to considerations of interpersonal utility dependencies. For any number of economic issues, the cost of considering them—though these costs are there—is not worth bearing. But when the issue is the existence and the proper treatment of merit goods, then such interpersonal utility dependencies cannot be ignored. Dealing with the fact that many people object strenuously to the commodification or to the commandification of some goods, and perhaps more often, to wealth distribution–dependent transactions in other goods, requires that these external moral costs be taken into account. For these costs are the bases for the legal structures that, in fact, exist, and, without considering such costs, little of any use can be said about these legal structures.

The problem, then, is not whether on occasion, or even frequently, economics properly excludes some tastes, values, and costs from consideration. It is what all too often can happen as a result of a lack of self-awareness of these exclusions and of the reasons for them. What too readily occurs is that, because economics often properly declines to consider such costs, many economists, and even more lawyer-economists, treat behavior, *in those contexts where such costs are central,* as inexplicable. And the move from that inexplicability to the totally inappropriate denomination of such behavior as irrational or as Pareto violative is a very small step that is too easily taken.

This, in turn, can lead to economics being treated as irrelevant to an analysis of the legal structures involved. But this, too, is wrong. I believe that an Economic Analysis of Law conclusion that a society's treatment of some merit goods is irrational or is Pareto violative is not worth the computer that develops it, the paper it is written on, if that conclusion derives from an analysis that ignores the existence of external moral costs when such costs, instead, are present and important. That does not mean, however, that economics may not be a very good, perhaps the best, source of examining and criticizing the legal structures that have been developed to deal with such merit goods.

Once economic theory realizes that in this context these costs cannot be excluded from the model, it is more than possible that an economic model will be developed that constitutes the best available way of criticizing, confirming, and perhaps reforming the legal structures currently used to deal with one or more merit goods. Such an economic model might, for example, point out—as to particular merit goods—that a modified market would be preferable to existing command allocations, or that a tax/subsidy approach would have significant advantages over a rationing structure that is currently being used, or *vice versa.* It might even support the conclusion that the particular good being treated as a merit one has a lower comparative

advantage in being so handled than would other goods not
currently included.

What Mill's criticism of Bentham suggested should be
done would come about![22] The law and economic mutual relationship would bear good fruit. The legal world's demand
that—in these instances—certain costs be made part of the
economic model would result in a more nuanced model. The
real world would not be dismissed as nonsense derived from
vague generalities, as might seem to occur if the economic
model that excluded those costs were employed. But the more
nuanced economic model would not simply rubber stamp the
legal world as it is. It would help lawmakers improve what had,
in unanalyzed ways, come to be. It would help us distinguish
between what, in those unanalyzed responses, was wisdom or
experience and what instead reflected surpassed notions, unnecessarily costly reactions, or exploitations by groups in
power.

The key to all this is, of course, more self-awareness resulting in openness and, dare I say it, greater honesty of treatment.
When economic theory chooses, for its own good reasons, to
ignore some values and costs, it must—*it must*—be aware that
it is doing so, and make that decision abundantly clear. It must
do so, that is, if it is properly to be taken seriously when employed in the task of analyzing law. And lawmakers must resist
relying, for their own political ends, on economic models that
further particular legal structures only because the models
ignore costs and values that are instead present. The task of the
law and economics scholar is to see to it that such openness and
honesty occur. It is also to ask for, and help develop, the more
nuanced, cost/value-inclusive economic theory.

The result of such law–economic interactions can be quite
wonderful. Coase's demand that economic theory take the costs

of markets into account not only helped explain the nature of firms but also helped in the analysis and reform of legal structures very far removed from those he was initially concerned with. Analogously, the need to consider the external moral costs that attach to the decision of the poor—because of their poverty—to volunteer for service in a limited war, and frequently to be killed, may lead to the development of an economic model that helps us to understand better how political campaign expenditures can best be dealt with.[23] And that, given the centrality of this question today and the complex issues of constitutional and legal process involved in it, would be quite an achievement. Once a model that considered such—to some extent interpersonal—utility dependencies were developed, its full usefulness could go way beyond what caused it to be demanded in the first place! Just as the effects of the introduction into economic models of the fact that both markets and command are costly (and I would add that modified markets and modified commands are costly, too) continue to startle and give insights in the most diverse of areas, so might the development of increasingly sophisticated economic models, models that began as ways of allowing lawyer-economists to deal better with the costs that have given rise to merit goods, bear unexpected and wonderful fruit elsewhere.

For this reason I end this essay—which may have seemed to begin on a negative note criticizing, and perhaps even berating, economics for not truly living up to its asserted taste/value neutrality—in a very optimistic way. The exclusion of some values, tastes, and resulting costs from some economic models is both understandable and justified. Open recognition and emphasis on what is excluded, and why, can lead to the demand for inclusion of such costs and values in those analyses where their exclusion renders the model of little use to the lawmaker.

And that demand can lead not only to the development of more inclusive models that may help improve the legal structures in the areas that gave rise to that demand, but also to an economic theory that serves as an Archimedean lever in law areas far removed.

But more can be asked of economics with respect to values and tastes! There are things that economists do better than almost anyone else that can give guidance—both to lawmakers and to scholars—as to what tastes and values can properly be said to be better, more desirable, than others. To this most startling and promising of issues, I now turn.[24]

VIII

Of Tastes and Values
What Economics Can Tell Us About Them

A.

There are few issues as important to law as the relationship between law and values. The laws and legal structures of a polity depend directly on the tastes and values of that polity. But the tastes and values of a society are themselves profoundly affected by the laws and legal structures that the society's lawmakers establish. There can be no doubt, for example, that the Supreme Court's decision in *Brown v. Board of Education,* however much it may have reflected changes in values since *Plessy v. Ferguson,* was highly instrumental in bringing about additional fundamental changes in our country's attitude toward race.[1] The same is true of the Massachusetts Supreme Court's decision in *Goodridge v. Dept. of Public Health*[2] with respect to same-sex marriage. And this again is so, both as to the decision's dependency on changed values, and its effect on furthering yet more changes.

As the *Goodridge* case shows, moreover, the effect is not always in one direction. A change in law can both accelerate the change in values that brought it about and give rise to powerful countermovements, sometimes permanently and sometimes just for a time.[3] This two-way effect on values is seen most dramatically, among recent cases, in *Roe v. Wade* and American attitudes toward abortion.[4] Sometimes, indeed, a reaction against a change in law, and the concomitant strengthening of opposing values, is more powerful than the change in values that the law-change sought to further. This may well have been the effect of the *Dred Scott* case.[5] By, in a sense, asserting that America was not to be half slave and half free, but all slave, *Dred Scott* changed the North's view of abolitionism radically. Abolition went from being viewed by many in the North as right, but not worth fighting over, to a cause that was broadly supported.[6]

The assertion of the centrality of lawmaking to the shaping of values, and hence of the necessity of taking that role of law into account, is one of the great achievements of the critical legal studies movement. I am all too aware of this because in my book *The Costs of Accidents,* in listing the various functions and aims of Torts Law, I—like most other writers on the subject—paid little or no heed to the crucial effect that branch of law has on what a society values and wants.[7] Torts, as much as any other area of law, affects our values, and it does so with respect to things as crucial as safety, the environment, the duty to look after each other, and life itself. In my earlier writings that relationship was at most implicitly noticed from time to time.[8] In my more recent writings, it has often been central to what I have said.[9] And I, like many other legal scholars whose work has been similarly influenced, have the critical legal scholars and their criticism to thank for this.

Sad to say, however, once the critical legal scholars pointed out the importance of taste- and value-shaping as a function of law, they had little more of a systematic sort to say about that function. Like most scholars, they commented on it and occasionally indicated how and in which direction laws did or were likely to shape tastes and values. (And that, as my adverting to *Brown v. Board of Education, Roe v. Wade,* and *Dred Scott* suggests, is certainly a useful thing to do.) But they, no more than anyone else, did much in the way of proposing analytical methods by which lawmakers could help gauge whether the changes in values that particular lawmakers wished to further or hinder were good, bad, or indifferent.

Sometimes—as I'll suggest at the end of this essay—legal scholars did make some analysis of why a specific legal rule might bring about a change in tastes or values that could, on the basis of that analysis, be deemed desirable. By and large though, both before and after the criticism of the critical legal scholars, the desirability or undesirability of modifications in values that changes in law were likely or intended to bring about, if treated at all, has been dealt with impressionistically or by naked assertion. Candid impressionistic treatments and forthright assertions of the goodness or badness of a change are, because of their openness, generally far better than analysis that simply ignores the law's effects on values. And openness may well be the most we can do. But the "Law and . . ." scholar must seek for more.

Indeed, it is manifest that many a field outside law, when used well, can say much about the merits and demerits of value changes. Not just the obvious subjects, like philosophy and theology, but many others, like history and literature, can tell us a great deal about the desirability or heinousness of the values that a particular change in law furthers. And, of course, these fields have both done so and have been, at least implicitly, relied upon by "Law and . . ." scholars in the past. My only comment on this at the moment is that, especially once one accepts the centrality of value formation to law, use of such fields should be both more systematic and more forthright than it often has been.

The question I want to ask here, however, is a different one: Does economics have a role to play in telling lawmakers what tastes and values are more desirable than others? Traditionally, as I mentioned before, economists have taken the position that they have nothing to say on the matter. Tastes and values are and must be, they assert, taken as a given, and economic analysis must work from there. *De gustibus non est disputandum*—concerning tastes there is nothing to be said—should be and (with whatever exceptions my last essay noted) is the rule. I will instead argue that economists, while remaining true to all the restrictions they have appropriately wanted to put on their field, can tell lawmakers a great deal about what value changes can properly be viewed as desirable. And I will also contend that they can do this on simple assumptions by employing those very skills that they and their field have more than anyone else. How can this be?

B.

Economists are, of course, correct that if we start with a totally blank slate—with no values or tastes at all—economics has nothing to say. It cannot tell us anything, including what initial tastes and values might be better than others; *ex nihilo nihil fit.* But if we assume even a minimal number of values—including one that economics regularly takes as a given, and another one that already features frequently in economic thought—then I believe that economics can tell us things about the relative desirability of subsidiary tastes and values that would be of great use to lawmakers.

To begin my analysis, I will assume that a society has just two values. First: more is better than less. Whatever pie is desired, a bigger pie is better than a smaller one. This assumption seems to me to be regularly made, indeed, to be taken for granted, in economics. Second: the society has a distributional preference with respect to the division of that pie. For my purposes here, what that distributional preference is does not matter. The result with respect to the desirability of particular value shaping will differ with different distributional preferences. But the capacity of economics to tell lawmakers what is desirable *given* that society's distributional preference is all that I am trying to establish. And, if you tell me *A,* then I can tell you that *B* follows, is something that economists do all the time. So, for my current purposes, I will assume no more than that a society can tell economists, or that economists can assume hypothetically, a preference for the division of the pie. In order to take the next step, I will here assume that that distributional preference is for equality; that a more equal distribution of the pie is preferable to a less equal one. But, as I said, the next step in my discussion can be taken assuming pretty much any distributional preference.

Taking these two preferences—more is better than less, and a more equal distribution is better than a less equal one—as givens, what can economists tell us about the desirability of subsidiary tastes? Quite a bit, I believe; any tastes or values that increase the desire for things which are in common supply in that society—for things that are not scarce—will yield a larger joint maximization of the two posited values. And any subsidiary tastes and values that cause people to want what is scarce, is rare, or requires particular effort to develop will lead to a lower joint maximization of the two assumed values. If people value and desire ordinary water and wine, and take pleasure in ordinary sport watching and ordinary sex—assuming, as I do, that these are commonly available—a high degree of satisfaction with a highly equal division of that satisfaction will follow. If people instead value and desire wines that are only produced with great difficulty, sport as performed by people with unusual physical attributes, and sex as manifested by people who have uncommon physical traits or capacities, then a much lower joint maximization is achieved. And a larger desired pie can only be made if that pie is unequally distributed.

To develop what is rare and make it available—to make it part of the pie—significant incentives, positive or negative, are needed. Those with the remarkable physical capacities— whether athletic or sexual—that I just mentioned must be induced to develop and manifest these capacities and make them available. This inducement, however, entails either, say, whipping them if they don't, or rewarding them munificently if they do make the capacities available. It requires positive or negative incentives in accordance to how much these people are specially able to satisfy the desire for that scarce attribute. And the whip or the million-dollar salary both necessarily result in a less equal distribution of the pie.

Since joint maximization analysis is something that economists not only do all the time, but are better at doing than most others, I believe this extremely simple example should suffice to establish a role for economists in advising lawmakers as to the relative desirability of different values and tastes. But, one might ask, how much can one really get from this? What actual laws and legal structures depend on this joint maximization analysis? Rather than answer that, I prefer to add one other simple taste or value to my list of "given," first-order preferences, and show that, with that very plausible addition, joint maximization analysis can directly speak to the desirability of fairly complex and important subsidiary values and of the laws that would further or hinder them.

That additional value is the desire to create.

Very many widely held religious traditions tell us that we are made in the image of the Creator.[10] Whether this statement is taken as truth or simply as an assertion of human attitudes, it does represent what I believe to be a very broad appreciation of, and desire for, creativity. It does not, it seems to me, require a great deal of speculation to posit a society in which people want (a) a larger rather than a smaller pie, (b) a particular division of that pie (I will again assume here a preference for a more equal division of the pie), and (c) to be individually creative in the making of that pie.

Given these assumptions, what can one say about joint maximization? Any set of subsidiary values and preferences that foster and give value to the ability to act creatively in ways that do not require scarce or unusual capacities will give rise to a larger and more equal amount of satisfaction than would occur if the subsidiary values and preferences are for creative activities that can be carried out only by those who have attributes that are scarce. Again, if the creativity that is wanted can be done by those who have skills or capacities analogous to the aforementioned rare sexual and athletic attributes, there will have to be incentives, positive or negative, and the satisfaction will suffer—in size or equality of division.

This conclusion, I hope to show, has immediate and significant consequences for the desirability of specific laws and legal structures. It causes us to ask two questions. First: What creative activities are broadly available to people who do not have unusual skills? Second: What can law do to further the desirability of such activities? The second goes to making the pie larger; the first, to making its division more equal.

An obvious answer for law and legal structures to the first question is the panoply of relatively informal artistic activities. Local choirs, karaoke, even singing in the shower could be examples. But so would handicrafts and such now often devalued arts like knitting, quilt making, and lacework. The relatively recent (in the United States) return of interest in really good home cooking is another, and not uninteresting example. In many European countries these activities have long been greatly appreciated. Is it silly to suggest that the statement, often made by Americans, that "people in those countries know how to live," actually takes notice of the fact that people in those countries value the above-mentioned set of widely available creative activities highly and, because of that—in this respect—enjoy a larger and more equally divided pie?

The same, of course, can be said for many things that Americans do appreciate. Local sports and local "do good" activities might qualify. When such activities, however, come to be viewed as trivial, and rather a waste of time in comparison to the same things done by professionals, that particular pie cannot be both large and relatively equally divided. I have no objection to great athletic feats. I am a Yankees fan and have long admired that team's superstars. I have less interest in the sexual prowess attributed, perhaps unrealistically, to some great cinematic and rock music performers. To the extent, however, that valuing these professionals devalues the same activities when done by ordinary people in ordinary places, it comes at an important cost in the joint maximization of satisfaction and its relatively equal distribution.

What has this to do with laws and legal structures? A great deal, as I hope to show by a more important example in a bit.

And, even as to these activities, it should be evident that desire for all of them can be furthered or lessened by legal rules. Laws can be passed that, both in direct effect and in subsidiary result, will lead people to value widely available creative activities more (or less) than those activities which require extraordinarily skillful and specially trained professionals. That is the lesson that, if we did not already know it, the critical legal scholars taught us.

There are, of course, great advantages to valuing what only specially qualified people can produce. And it should be no surprise that laws are passed, and structures are created, that further the desire for these relatively scarce products. The above discussion—which derives from the simplest of economic analyses—suggests, however, that whatever those benefits are, they come at a cost. Absent such analysis, these costs might not be adequately appreciated. Since intelligent lawmaking should take these "value-alteration" costs into account, the making of that analysis is worthwhile. And that analysis, not only in the simple form that I have proffered but also in far more complex variants of it, is one that economics is most suited to do.

C.

There is today, moreover, an important example of the potential conflict between the continued high valuation of a widely available creative activity, and the furthering, through laws and legal structures, of values that can all too readily lead to a depreciation of this nonscarce creative activity. I am referring to child rearing. Bringing up children involves much drudgery, but it is also highly creative and can give the satisfaction rewards that accrue when a desire to be creative is fulfilled. It is also an activity that a very large proportion of the population can engage in. At the same time, it is an activity that traditionally was assigned to women. And this assignment was part and parcel of, I do not hesitate to say it, the awful discrimination against women that characterizes our societies.[11]

My first premise is that it is manifestly desirable to end that discrimination. My second premise is that laws and legal systems can be extremely important in ridding us of that bigotry, as they have been in moving us away from racial and religious biases. Indeed, recent legal changes have occurred that are designed to do just that: diminishing the bias directly through prohibitions and rules and indirectly by furthering value changes that make that bias less acceptable, even apart from rules.

I would suggest, however, that in doing this we may have, in a literal sense, been care-less and thought-less of the fact that there are various ways of ridding us of these deeply rooted discriminatory values. One seemingly easy way of reducing this bias has, I fear, ignored the very joint maximization costs that I have been discussing. It has acted by diminishing the value, the appreciation, that is given to child rearing. It has made ordinary, out-of-home, but not especially creative, jobs available to women and furthered legal structures that implied that holding a paying job is worth doing, while staying home and rearing children is not. This has promoted equality—and has done so in the way most commonly done—by making available to a dominated group what was previously stereotypically done only by the dominant group.[12] It sought to achieve equality by treating women like men, and since men traditionally did not look after children, it downgraded that occupation.

Doing this, of course, entails costs to the children. But these could be attenuated. Children could perhaps be still brought up, and maybe very well, by highly specialized child-rearers, or schools.[13] And what I am concerned with in this essay is less with the—albeit very important—question of how well children are reared than with the fact that such an approach to equality means devaluing—and hence removing from most people the ability to engage in a *valued* creative activity—child rearing. Of course, some women could remain home and look after children. But their creativity—in my hypothetical— would be little valued. Others could go into the world of work and engage in jobs that all too often in our societal structure, though remunerated and even valued, are not in any way creative. The resulting pie—given my three simple original value preferences—would either be smaller or less equally divided than could be achieved by a different way of furthering male– female equality.

Contrast all this with laws that promote the view that staying home and looking after children is a crucially valuable societal activity. Whether furthering such an appreciation for the "upbringing of the next generation" would require, or be helped by, paying those who did this, or whether it could readily be done in other ways, is beyond my immediate concern.[14] But one way or another—to the extent that laws and legal structures have an effect on value formation—a society could enact laws that promote the desirability of engaging in child rearing. That same society could also, and contemporaneously, make clear through its laws and structures that both *this* highly prized activity *and* outside jobs are available and properly done by males and females alike. The result would be the appreciation of a highly creative activity that is available not only to a few. And a higher level of joint maximization (a) of satisfaction and (b) of relative equality of distribution of that satisfaction (given the assumed desire to create) would thereby be accomplished.

D.

If, on the basis of such very rudimentary value assumptions, a simple economic joint maximization model can lead to results that can have such immediate relevance to a highly significant legal question that we face today, is it unduly optimistic to believe that analogous and more complex work by economists can help criticize, confirm, and reform our laws and lawmaking? I don't believe it is. It would not in any way violate the rigor of economic analysis, or its relative neutrality, for economists or lawyer-economists to look at their society and empirically conclude: This society has four or five "fundamental values"; four or five things to which it adheres deeply. A fair amount of agreement as to what these are can, I think, be fairly easily achieved in most societies. And, starting from such "original values," economists could then develop some extraordinarily interesting joint maximization models based on the relationship of various subsidiary values to these fundamental ones.

Determining which subsidiary values would help or would hinder the joint maximization of the fundamental values would be of direct and crucial significance to legal scholars and to lawmakers. For it would ask them to consider which laws and which legal structures would foster the subsidiary values that would, in the above sense, be desirable and which would impede them. And this, in turn, would cause lawyers—again, with the help of economists—to consider what other costs and benefits would attach to legal structures that promoted the desirable subsidiary values. Significantly, doing all this would tell us, in a scholarly way and using the tools of economics in ways that are not very different from what economists and lawyers do all the time, an immense amount about the desirability of different laws and legal structures. It would, in other words, help answer the question the critical legal scholarship movement made clear we should ask, but then left hanging.

E.

I want, however, to suggest an even broader role for economists in this area. I would like to encourage economists to go beyond the empirical work of trying to discern what a given society values fundamentally and then deriving the consequences of those original values for subsidiary values and for lawmaking. I would like economists, or at least lawyer-economists, to be willing to say, openly: There are four or five fundamental values that *I* believe are worthy. I would like scholars to be willing to make such fundamental *value* assumptions and then work out the consequences of those assumptions. As to these openly asserted, posited values, the same questions would be asked: what subsidiary values, and what legal structures fostering these subsidiary values, would further their joint maximization and what are the other benefits, and *costs,* of such legal structures?

Doing this may seem dangerous to economists; it might seem to move them beyond the value neutrality that they have often sought after and asserted. But in fact, some of the oldest and greatest economists have done things of just this sort in widely different economic contexts.[15] And, as I suggested in my last essay, I believe that there have been any number of values that—in economics and in Law and Economics—we have been all too willing, silently, to treat as not there or not worth considering. Why not do the opposite and do it openly?

What if economists and lawyer-economists were willing to say: *If* this society cares about *A, B, C, D,* and *E*—and we think it should—then subsidiary values *F, G, H, I, J, K, L,* and *M* would lead to the higher joint maximization of these fundamental values. And we believe that laws and legal structures X, Y, and Z would lead to people having the above listed subsidiary values and, hence, to be desirable. Such a statement would both use the tools that economics has, and be scholarly. Whether that scholarship turned out to be useful or not would depend on whether any given polity agreed with the scholar as to the accuracy and importance of the fundamental values that the scholar posited. But there is nothing wrong or unscholarly or unrigorous about that. And, if it were done and done openly, it would put that scholar—and the economics that scholar practiced—at the very center of lawmaking and criticizing; it would make Law and Economics both relevant and essential.

I do not want to overstate. The actual relationship between laws and values is immensely complicated. Do laws designed or intended to further values do so, or do they bring a counterreaction? That is often hard to say. Can other values that (for noneconomic reasons) a society wishes to further, in fact, be achieved, while also accomplishing what the economists' joint maximization analysis suggests should be done? And even if these other societal values can coexist with those that are brought to full light as a result of the economic analysis that I have been suggesting, what is the additional cost of that coexistence? Lawmaking, especially when it involves value formation, is very hard. And as Arthur Corbin reminded us long ago, what any outside leverage point can add to that process is limited.[16]

But economics has proven itself to be immensely helpful—both in its straight Economic Analysis of Law manifestation and through the reciprocal relationship I have called Law and Economics—to the criticism, confirmation, and reform of any number of legal areas. So far, it has not even tried to help in this most crucial of legal issues—value analysis. I believe I have shown that it has something significant to contribute here. When I, among others, long ago suggested that economics had much to say about law, some of the leading legal scholars of the time scoffed. They said that is not law or legal scholarship. We said, in effect, wait and see, you may be surprised.[17] And so it turned out. I say the same today about economics and the legal analysis of value formation. Wait and see. For myself, I believe it to be as important a future area for the interplay of law and economics as those first suggestions that some of us made some fifty-five years ago turned out to be.

There is no point in belaboring the issue. The underlying challenge throughout this essay remains the same. There are questions as to which legal rule making needs help. They involve values, attitudes, tastes, and their changes. The skills that economists have render economists particularly capable of giving lawmakers help. Yet applying these skills in such areas requires a willingness for economists to do certain things that they traditionally have been reluctant to do. The indications of what value changes induced by law are desirable need not require—as some might argue—a greater tolerance of fuzziness. But they do demand that the doer of this kind of analysis postulate or assume, for any given society, a limited number of core values whose interrelation and joint maximization economic analysis can then address. I can understand the reluctance of economists to do this. But the benefits of overcoming such hesitations and of focusing on this area of joint maximization are so great that I hope that economists will overcome any reluctance. And once they have done so, and have devised any number of variants on what I have adverted to here, I am sure that they will bring forth important results which go well beyond those that I can already perceive.

The world of legal institutions, as viewed and analyzed by legal scholars, frequently reflects the fact that current economic theory is not adequate to explain existing legal institutions in any given society. The prevalence and treatment of altruism, of merit goods, as well as much of the law of torts and of eminent domain in the United States, are but three examples. That same legal world cries out for guidance from economic theory in assessing what subsidiary laws and values are of help in giving optimal recognition to the fundamental values of the relevant society. Economists, working with legal scholars, can, by making economic theory richer and more nuanced, make that theory more capable of responding to both of these needs. They can do so without abandoning those limits that economics has traditionally, and understandably, placed on itself in order to retain its rigor. Law and Economics scholarship has done this to wonderful effect in the past. But there is much still to be done, and it is this that makes the future of Law and Economics so bright and exciting to me, an early tiller in the field.

Appendix

Farewell Letter of Arthur Corbin to the Yale
Law School Faculty

Nearly all of you have been my students; and I am sure that you do not need to be told that I have always enjoyed my work with you—38 years of question and answer in the classroom, of lingering discussion after class, of personal contact in the office—38 years in one profession and in one law school, having had contact with seven deans, having been part of at least three faculty generations, working to make this school hold its own in competition with the best.

To construct a theory of law and its evolutionary development, to build up a student body of selected college graduates, to get and to hold a faculty of full-time teachers and producing scholars, to turn out men and books and a Yale Law Journal that would win respect and influence in the world: these have been my prevailing aims and ambitions.

The Common Law is not "a brooding omnipresence in the sky," said Oliver Wendell Holmes. In spite of this warning, all of us, including the great Justice himself, seem continually to search for the absolute—even though we know that nothing that is man-made can be absolute. We look for absolute rules and principles of law. We hope that by historical research, in the Year Books and Reports, we can find them—somewhere back in the origins of the Common Law. What was the true consideration for a promise? With some sadness, perhaps, we discover that this process gives no key to the door of absolute wisdom and eternal justice—the justice, as Cardozo put it, "that would declare itself by tokens plainer and more commanding than its place and glimmering reflections in my own vacillating mind and conscience"—the illusory justice that Woodrow Wilson said he went to find at the Peace Conference only 22 years ago, "a peace of justice, not a mere balancing of interests."

Disillusioned in this search, do we accept our own human limitations and content ourselves with less? We do not. Admitting, as our latest discovery, that there are no principles, that there is no law, we turn to fields with other names—to economics, ethics, political science. Surely here we can find our absolutes, our eternal principles of right and of justice. Some of us may go back and back, to St. Thomas, and to Aristotle, to find and to swallow their stated absolutes. The less we know of economics and ethics and politics, the more likely we are to enjoy the illusion that in them we find certainty, or at least the illusion that certainty is just around the corner. But just as in the field called Law, that corner is never turned. The fact is that these are merely different names for a single field—the field of human experience.

I believe that there is greater hope, of human welfare and happiness, if we are conscious of our limitations, if we abandon the quest for absolutes, if we confess that justice is wholly relative and human, and if we erect our temple of peace upon a foundation, made as stable as we can by a neat balancing of interests, determined by as careful and complete a study of human experience as is possible.

Rules and principles, where we call them political, economic, ethical or legal, are the result of this balancing of interests. They are the tentative working rules of life—not to be scorned because they are not absolute. They are all we have, to guide our own footsteps into the unknown future. If they are ill-made, by the ignorant, the cocksure, and the reckless, they will indeed mislead us. The great benefactor is one who can make them well, a man who collects and analyses and compares the case experiences of life, and can draw therefrom a reasonable working rule. Our misfortune is that we have so many Doctors of the absolute, and so few such masters of inductive social science.

I have always believed that the most important part, in the evolution of our legal system, is played by the judges. The part played by juries and lawyers and legislators must not be under-estimated. Nor must that played by the professors. The work of the professors is a necessary work, and may be increasing in its importance. We are the midwives who start the infant lawyer and jurist on his way. We are the gadflies that sting judges into better action. We are, of necessity, the generalizers, and the critics of the generalizations that the judges make to justify their decisions. But the judges *make* decisions. The professors make *none*. If the professors assume a position of critical superiority over the work of the judges, it is very often a false assumption. It is indeed an *easy* and *maybe* a *fatuous* assumption. We have the last word, in our law magazines and our classrooms. We are the Monday morning quarterbacks. We are the *observers* of the vital work of other men. We do not carry the weight of responsibility for the lives and fortunes of clients as do practicing lawyers and the judges. We have no pair of opposing counsel, eying us with argumentative zeal, prepared to test the rules that we lay down and the statements that we make, ready to nullify our words and acts by appeal to a higher court.

It is true that we do have critics in front of us—a lot of bright young folk who may *wonder* at our assumption of omniscience and may *smile* at our fatuousness. These are indeed critics to be respected. But they are not yet well prepared to test our generalizations; and in several other ways we have them at a disadvantage. We can flatter them into joining *with* us in an assumed critical superiority; we can overawe them by threat of examinations and poor recommendations; and we can bore them into total indifference.

In view of your kindly treatment of me tonight I am not going to take advantage of you any longer in these ways. Besides, if I should bore you longer I fear that you would *not show* indifference. Therefore, I shall close with one more expression of my affectionate regards and of my gratitude at your having given me so good a job for so long a period.

Notes

1
Of Law and Economics and Economic Analysis of Law

1. John Stuart Mill, *Bentham, in* Mill on Bentham and Coleridge 39, 59 (F. R. Leavis ed., 1980).

2. While I differentiate between "Economic Analysis of Law" and "Law and Economics," others do not. *See, e.g.,* Robert Cooter & Thomas Ulen, Law and Economics (6th ed. 2012). Still others differentiate in ways very different from me. *See, e.g.,* Alain Mariano & Giovanni B. Ramello, *Consent, Choice, and Guido Calabresi's Heterodox Economic Analysis of Law,* 77 Law & Contemp. Prob. 97, 97–98 (2014).

3. Mill, *supra* note 1, at 59.

4. Guido Calabresi & A. Douglas Melamed, *Property Rules, Liability Rules, and Inalienability: One View of the Cathedral,* 85 Harv. L. Rev. 1089 (1972).

5. *Spur v. Del Webb* was decided soon after; it was and still is a very unusual instance. *See* Spur Indus., Inc. v. Del E. Webb Dev. Co., 494 P.2d 700 (1972) (en banc).

6. For example, we noted numerous instances in which eminent domain functions in this very same way. *See Calabresi & Melamed, supra* note 4, at 1117, n.58.

7. For example, Daniel Kahneman and Amos Tversky have demonstrated that the way in which decisions are framed or choices are labeled leads to persistent violations of the principle of invariance—"different representations of the same choice problem should yield the same preference"—previously

thought to be an essential element of rational decision making. Amos Tversky & Daniel Kahneman, *Rational Choice and the Framing of Decisions,* J. Bus., Oct. 1986, at 251, 253–62.

To illustrate, consider the following trivial, personal example: Upon graduation from Yale College in 1953, my roommates and I purchased several bottles of that year's vintage of Chateau Mouton Rothschild to put aside for a later reunion. Twenty-five years later, the wine was considered one of the greats of the century and sold for thousands of dollars a bottle. We all decided to enjoy the wine with some former classmates, though we never would have purchased the wine at that price. From a traditional economic standpoint, there should have been no difference between buying bottles in 1978 for thousands of dollars or drinking the same bottles that we had purchased in 1953.

Even in earlier work, Kahneman and Tversky had identified numerous cognitive biases not accounted for by traditional economic theory. *See, e.g.,* Amos Tversky & Daniel Kahneman, *Judgment Under Uncertainty: Heuristics and Biases,* 185 Sci. 1124 (1974).

8. *See, e.g.,* Ward Farnsworth, *Do Parties to Nuisance Suits Bargain After Judgment? A Glimpse Inside the Cathedral,* 66 U. Chi. L. Rev. 373 (1999); *see also,* Benjamin Shmueli & Yuval Sinai, *Calabresi's and Maimonides's Tort Law Theories—A Comparative Analysis and a Preliminary Sketch of a Modern Model of Differential Pluralistic Tort Liability Based on the Two Theories,* 26 Yale J. L. & Human. (2014); Benjamin Shmueli, *What Have Calabresi & Melamed Got to Do with Family Affairs? Women Using Tort Law in Order to Defeat Jewish and Shari'a Law,* 25 Berkeley J. Gender L. & Just. 125 (2010).

9. Some have recently criticized behavioral economics as losing its broader aims and becoming too insular with respect to the noneconomic disciplines from which insight may be gleaned. *See, e.g.,* Owen D. Jones, *Why Behavioral Economics Isn't Better, and How It Could Be, in* Research Handbook on Behavioral Law and Economics (J. Teitelbaum & K. Zeiler eds., forthcoming 2015). I believe that those who originated the field set out to do the broadest such work. Not only did they seek to base behavioral economics on psychology and neuroscience, but they also used these to explain why the real world did not fit existing economic models. And this larger aim of capturing that interplay between the real world and theory is what I stress here as the proper future agenda of Law and Economics.

10. Guido Calabresi & Philip Bobbitt, Tragic Choices (1978).

11. *Id.* at 134–43 (describing the first-order sufficiency paradox in terms of its ability both to render certain tragic choices life-validating, despite their negative effects in other tragic contexts, and to make certain other tragic choices as *not* life-negating despite their directly or indirectly life-taking effects).

12. *See id.* at 21, 40, 221 n.2 (giving, as examples, our willingness as a society to spend vast sums to save a downed balloonist or a hostage, and the willingness of a mining company to pay extravagantly to save a few trapped miners but not to spend comparatively less to save more lives through better safety precautions). I have elsewhere given the example of "spending millions to save fools who choose to cross the Atlantic in a rowboat," but not to spend the same amount or less on safety precautions that would save far more lives. Guido Calabresi, *The Complexity of Torts—The Case of Punitive Damages, in* EXPLORING TORT LAW 333, 342–43 (M. Stuart Madden ed., 2005); *see also* Guido Calabresi, *Commentary: Kenneth J. Arrow, in* ETHICS OF HEALTH CARE: PAPERS OF THE CONFERENCE ON HEALTH CARE AND CHANGING VALUES 48, 53 (Lawrence R. Tancredi ed., 1973) ("Thus a dramatic decision to spend millions of dollars to save a fool who has chosen to row across the Atlantic has external benefits, which spending much less money to make a highway safer—with far greater lifesaving effect—apparently does not.").

13. *See, e.g.,* Michael Faure, *Calabresi and Behavioural Tort Law and Economics,* 1 ERASMUS L. REV. 75, 75 (2008) ("This paper illustrates how Guido Calabresi was already aware of cognitive limits: for instance, concerning the ability of parties to assess how much they should spend 'for their own good'. This led him to arrive at balanced conclusions with regard to normative consequences of these limits. Many of the ideas of behavioural law and economics were hence already implicit in Calabresi's writings."). For the fact that it was perplexing *see, e.g.,* Kenneth Arrow, *Modes of Choice,* 88 YALE L.J. 436, 436 (1978) (reviewing CALABRESI & BOBBITT, TRAGIC CHOICES) ("Reading [*Tragic Choices*] is an experience that is both fascinating and frustrating. It is very like crossing a rocky unfamiliar terrain at night in a lightning storm. All sorts of new perceptions appear with blinding clarity. But it is difficult to draw a map afterwards showing others where one has been.").

14. CALABRESI & BOBBIT, *supra* note 10, at 77, n.46 (citing Margaret Mead in a discussion of the "worthiness" approach to dealing with tragic choices).

15. Indeed, this may be one reason the Yale Law School has recently begun offering a Ph.D. in law. Doing scholarship in "Law and . . ." does not always require the intense and highly specialized work in one discipline that would be required if one were to complete a Ph.D. in that discipline. The Ph.D. in law may allow interdisciplinary study and dialogue sufficient to meet the needs of lawyer-economists, lawyer-anthropologists, or lawyer-philosophers, or of some combination of these.

16. Mill's forceful call for equality of the sexes is but one well-known example. *See* JOHN STUART MILL, *The Subjugation of Women, in* ON LIBERTY AND OTHER ESSAYS 471–583 (John Gray ed., Oxford Univ. Press 1991) (1869).

17. The later work of Frank Michelman has recently been characterized as embodying precisely this interplay between philosophy and law. *See* Robert Post, *Provocation: Frank's Way*, 125 Harv. L. Rev. Forum 218, 226 (2012) ("Frank knows that agreement—that is to say opinion—is indispensable to political governance, and therefore to law. He is thus drawn to conclude that legitimacy itself can be based upon opinion, and not solely upon the exercise of philosophical reason. Although Frank begins with the thought that the respect-worthiness of a regime depends upon the truth of the contents of its human rights, he is inevitably led to the distinct conclusion that a regime cannot be respect-worthy unless it is responsive to the freely formed opinion of its people. . . . Frank has shifted from the question of philosophical truth to the question of political legitimacy. Frank has crossed the border from philosophy into law.").

18. I have elsewhere described the basic characteristics of formalism in greater detail. *See* Guido Calabresi, *An Introduction to Legal Thought: Four Approaches to Law and to the Allocation of Body Parts*, 55 Stan. L. Rev., 2113, 2113–18 (2003). *See also,* Ernest J. Weinrib, The Idea of Private Law 12–13 (1995) ("[P]rivate law strives to avoid contradiction, to smooth out inconsistencies, and to realize a self-adjusting harmony of principles, rules, and standards. . . . Internal to the process of the law is the incremental transformation or reinterpretation or even the repudiation of specific decisions so as to make them conform to a wider pattern of coherence. In the classic phrase of common law lawyers, the law can work itself pure.").

The inherently conservative nature of legal formalism has at times, however, paradoxically served liberal ends. In Italy, for example, scholars opposing Fascism were formalists who used the self-contained nineteenth-century formalistic system as "a great weapon" against Fascism, for that system conserved "the liberal, nineteenth-century political approach, as well as nineteenth-century economic laissez-faire," and, most important, "basic democratic attitudes." Guido Calabresi, *Two Functions of Formalism: In Memory of Guido Tedeschi,* 67 U. Chi. L. Rev. 479, 482 (2000).

19. Following its near extinction in 1869, the Yale Law School sought to refashion itself as the premier institution of interdisciplinary legal studies, with a greater emphasis on public law and other disciplines, by integrating itself more fully with Yale College. This shift was partly born of necessity, as the law school was short on resources and could not hope, it believed, to compete with Columbia Law School (the leading law school of the time) in hiring legal scholars. Thus, Yale Law School began to supplement courses taught by local legal practitioners with courses taught by members of the Yale College faculty in the hopes, as its Dean at the time stated, to " 'be regarded as

the place of instruction in all sound learning relating to the foundations of justice, the history of law . . . the constitution . . . the law of nations . . . finance and taxation,' political theory, and comparative law." JOHN H. LANGBEIN, HISTORY OF THE YALE LAW SCHOOL: THE TERCENTENARY LECTURES 64 (with A. Kronman et al.) (2004).

20. For a detailed account of the relationship between Pound, Hohfeld, and Corbin, *see* N. E. HULL, ROSCOE POUND, & KARL LLEWELLYN: SEARCH-ING FOR AN AMERICAN JURISPRUDENCE, 97–116 (1997).

21. *See, e.g.,* Roscoe Pound, *The Scope and Purpose of Sociological Juris-prudence,* 24 HARV. L. REV. 591 (1911); ROSCOE POUND, 1 JURISPRUDENCE 349 (1959) ("The science of law of today . . . has given over its exclusiveness and seeks what may be called team play with the other social sciences.").

22. *See* Calabresi, *supra* note 18, at 2142 (arguing that while different "Law and . . ." approaches look to guidance in very different places, "the un-derlying approach would be the same, however, in its view of the role both of legal scholarship and of the legal scholar. It would be identical regardless of what the 'Law and . . .' school was, and it would be totally different from the methods used by the doctrinalists.").

23. *See, e.g.,* ARTHUR CORBIN, CORBIN ON CONTRACTS (1952); Arthur Corbin, *Principles of Law and Their Evolution,* 64 YALE L.J. 161, 161–63 (1954).

24. R. H. Coase, *The Nature of the Firm,* 4 ECONOMICA 386 (1937).

25. As we will see later, *see infra* Chapter 5, Section B, it is significant that Coase, in comparing the command structure underlying firms with costly markets, was *not* comparing a pure, centralized, governmental command structure, but a private, decentralized—i.e., modified—one.

26. R. H. Coase, *The Problem of Social Cost,* 3 J.L. & ECON. 1 (1960).

27. Richard Posner, *The Economic Approach to Law,* 3 TEX. L. REV. 757, 759 (1975).

28. HARRY SHULMAN & FLEMING JAMES, JR., CASES AND MATERIALS ON THE LAW OF TORTS (1st ed., 1942).

29. Guido Calabresi, *Some Thoughts on Risk Distribution and the Law of Torts,* 70 YALE L.J. 499 (1961).

30. While the Coase article is dated 1960, before mine, *The Problem of Social Cost* was in fact not published until 1961, that is, after my article had been published. I was thus unaware of it when I wrote my article. *See* Richard Posner, *Guido Calabresi's* The Cost of Accidents*: A Reassessment,* 64 MD. L. REV. 12, 13 n.6 (2005).

I say Coase's article was greater because while my article did much that could be called Law and Economics, and while I did suggest that in some situations a particular "cost" (for example, automobile–pedestrian accidents) could not be viewed as caused by one activity (e.g., driving), but rather by both (walking and driving), Calabresi, *supra* note 29, at 506, n.24, I did not spell out that causal symmetry as fully as Coase did. Further, and most important, Coase's explicit discussion of the internalization of externalities was missing from my piece.

31. Recent work, however, has examined this period with a fresh perspective. *See, e.g.,* Steven G. Medema, Juris *Prudence: Calabresi's Uneasy Relationship with the Coase Theorem,* 77 Law & Contemp. Probs. 65, 85 (2014) (discussing the interaction between me, Blum and Kalven, and Coase); Alain Marciano, *Accident Costs, Resource Allocation and Individual Rationality: Blum, Kalven, and Calabresi, in* Annual Conference, European Society for the History of Economic Thought (2014); Alain Marciano, *Guido Calabresi's Economic Analysis of Law, Coase and the Coase Theorem,* 32 Int'l Rev. L. & Econ. 110, 118 (2012).

32. *See* Walter J. Blum & Harry Kalven, *Public Law Perspectives on a Private Law Problem,* 31 U. Chi. L. Rev. 641 (1964); Guido Calabresi, *Fault, Accidents, and the Wonderful World of Blum and Kalven,* 75 Yale L.J. 216 (1965); Walter J. Blum & Harry Kalven, Jr., *The Empty Cabinet of Dr. Calabresi: Auto Accidents and General Deterrence,* 34 U. Chi. L. Rev. 239 (1967).

33. *See, e.g.,* Harold Demsetz, *Toward a Theory of Property Rights,* Am. Econ. Rev., May 1967, at 347–59; Harold Demsetz, *When Does the Rule of Liability Matter?,* 1 J. Legal. Stud. 13 (1972). *See also* Harold Demsetz, *Toward a Theory of Property Rights II: The Competition Between Private and Collective Ownership,* 31 J. Legal. Stud. 653 (2002).

34. *See* Calabresi, *supra* note 29, at 543–45.

35. Guido Calabresi, The Costs of Accidents: A Legal and Economic Analysis (1970).

36. Frank I. Michelman, *Pollution as a Tort: A Non-Accidental Perspective on Calabresi's Costs,* 80 Yale L.J. 647 (1971) (book review).

37. *See* Calabresi & Melamed, *supra* note 4. For my own reconsideration of that article, *see infra* Chapter 6.

38. Richard A. Posner, *Book Review,* 37 U. Chi. L. Rev. 636, 636 (1970) (reviewing Guido Calabresi, The Cost of Accidents: A Legal and Economic Analysis [1970]). Amusingly, Posner began his review by writing, "Torts is not my field. But in one sense, neither is it Guido Calabresi's"—this because of my unusual use of economics in examining tort law. Needless to say, Posner soon changed his mind as to the relationship between law and economics.

39. *See e.g.,* Richard Posner, Economic Analysis of Law (1973); Richard Posner, The Economics of Justice (1983); Richard Posner,

An Economic Approach to Legal Procedure and Judicial Administration, 2 J. LEG. STUD. 399 (1973); William M. Landes and Richard Posner, *An Economic Analysis of Copyright Law,* 18 J. LEG. STUD. 325 (1989).

40. In the fall of 1960, I was invited by Dean Edward Levi to interview at the University of Chicago. Ahead of my December meeting there, I circulated a copy of the soon to be published *Some Thoughts* to the Chicago faculty. Though the version of the article did not include a full discussion of the reciprocity of causation, *see supra* note 30, it nonetheless provoked some controversy. I was greeted on the train platform in Chicago by Harry Kalven, who was waving a copy of the article saying, "It's wrong, wrong, wrong, but I wish I'd written something as wrong." *See* Laura Kalman, *Some Thoughts on Yale and Guido,* 77 LAW & CONTEMP. PROBS. 15, 39 (2014). Later, I met with Aaron Director, who asked me if I knew of Coase. I replied that I had read Coase's 1959 article, *The Federal Communications Commission,* but didn't see what it could possibly have to do with *Some Thoughts.* It wasn't until *The Problem of Social Cost* appeared soon after that I realized what Director—who had already edited Coase's piece—was referring to. Kalman, *supra,* at 39–40.

41. *See, e.g.,* ROBERT BORK, THE ANTITRUST PARADOX (1978); Richard Posner, *The Chicago School of Antitrust Analysis,* 127 U. PA. L. REV. 925 (1978). *See generally,* W. KIP VISCUSI, JOSEPH E. HARRINGTON, JR., & JOHN M. VERNON, ECONOMICS OF REGULATION AND ANTITRUST (4th ed. 2005).

42. *See, e.g.,* STEVEN SHAVELL, FOUNDATIONS OF ECONOMIC ANALYSIS OF LAW (2009).

43. *See, e.g.,* CALABRESI, *supra* note 35.

44. *See* MILL, *supra* note 16.

45. *See, e.g,* Guido Calabresi, Lecture at the University College of Turin: History and Meaning of Law and Economics (Jan. 24, 2012), *available at* http://www.youtube.com/watch?v=UDz8R_PhscY.

46. Richard Posner, *The Economic Approach to Law,* 53 TEX. L. REV. 657, 774–75 (1975).

47. The value of an outside perspective has been dramatically shown by the work in psychology that led to behavioral economics. *See supra* note 7.

48. *See, e.g.,* Philip Mirowski, *The Philosophical Bases of Institutionalist Economics,* 21 J. ECON. ISS. 1001, 1028 (1987) (noting growing attacks by neoclassical economists from the 1930s to the 1960s against institutionalists for being "unscientific"). For an extensive account of the roots of the struggle between neoclassical and institutional economists, *see* YUVAL P. YONAY, THE STRUGGLE OVER THE SOUL OF ECONOMICS: INSTITUTIONALIST AND NEOCLASSICAL ECONOMISTS IN AMERICA BETWEEN THE WARS (1998).

49. As I have written elsewhere, "Perhaps because of Coase's [then] socialism, *The Nature of the Firm* emphasized the costs of markets and pointed out that when nonmarket (i.e. command or hierarchical) structures could accomplish desired results at lower costs, people would organize themselves into such structures—for example, firms or even governments—in order better to achieve those results. Perhaps because Coase had become a libertarian, *The Problem of Social Cost* emphasized the possible benefits of markets. It pointed out that when transaction costs were not prohibitive, people would enter into transactions creating markets, not only to get around 'inefficient' hierarchical or command structures, but also to fill the vacuum left by the absence of preexisting market or command relationships." Guido Calabresi, *The Pointlessness of Pareto: Carrying Coase Further,* 100 YALE L.J. 1211, 1212 (1991).

In his comments at a conference commemorating the fiftieth anniversary of *The Nature of the Firm,* held at Yale University on May 14–16, 1987, under the auspices of the Economics of Organization program of the Yale University School of Organization and Management, Professor Coase mentioned that he was a socialist at the time he wrote the article. In the published version of his comments at the Yale conference, however, Coase mentions that, while he was a socialist when he first decided to study economics, his "basic approach" in *The Nature of the Firm* was given to him by the teachings of Arnold Plant. Ronald Coase, *The Nature of the Firm: Origin,* 4 J.L. ECON. & ORG. 3, 5, 7 (1988). He then states that he never felt any need to reconcile his socialist sympathies with an acceptance of Plant's approach: "In my case my socialist views fell away fairly rapidly without any obvious stage of rejection." *Id.* at 8. Thus, in his published version of the conference lecture, Coase suggests that he may no longer have been much of a socialist when he wrote *The Nature of the Firm. Cf.* George L. Priest, *Ronald Coase, Firms and Markets* (John M. Olin Center Research Paper No. 510, Sept. 2014) (arguing that Coase's views changed sharply from supporting government management in *Nature of the Firm* to endorsing unfettered markets in *The Problem of Social Cost*).

50. In the early years after it was published, *The Problem of Social Cost* was often criticized for being little more than "right-wing" ideology. *See, e.g.,* Edmund W. Kitch, *The Fire of Truth: A Remembrance of Law and Economics at Chicago, 1932–1970,* 26 J.L. & ECON. 163, 226 (1983) ("There was an enormous amount of criticism of the social cost article when it was published. Dozens of refutations were written, some of which were never printed."). In this sense, it is unfortunate that discussion of the reciprocity of causation was not as prominent in my article *Some Thoughts on Risk Distribution and*

the Law of Torts as it had been in an earlier draft. For reasons I've discussed elsewhere, I was eventually talked out of including the fuller discussion. *See* Guido Calabresi, *Commentary on Some Thoughts on Risk Distribution and the Law of Torts,* 100 YALE L.J. 1482, 1484 (1991). That point, however, was one of the most contentious in Coase's article, and had my article been as clear in taking the same position as Coase with regard to the reciprocity of causation, such attacks would have been considerably different given my then liberal (i.e. interventionistic) point of view, as reflected in *Some Thoughts* as a whole. Today, it is much harder to view the Coase Theorem as an ideology rather than as a scholarly position. Much ink could have been spared had that been seen earlier. *But see* Priest, *supra* note 49 (arguing that Coase was also taking a strong libertarian position).

51. The principal reason appellate-court decisions rarely dealt with "reverse damages" has to do with the free-rider problem. If, for instance, an entitlement to abate the nuisance created by a polluting coal plant were granted (but also required compensation to the nuisancor), it is likely that many in the affected community would not join in litigation against the plant, hoping that some would sue, and pay the damages, while they could benefit from the abatement without bearing any costs. All too often, this means no abatement suit is brought. *Spur* is the rare exception. In that case, the Arizona Supreme Court enjoined a cattle feedlot operator (Spur Industries) from continuing its operations near a planned residential development. *See Spur,* 494 P.2d at 705–6. The Court, however, also required the plaintiff-developer (Del E. Webb Development Co.) to compensate Spur for the costs of relocation. *Id.* at 706–7. The unusual facts of the case mitigated the free-rider problem. Del Webb, as the developer, was big enough to take on the costs of the litigation and resulting compensation to Spur, while spreading the costs to future purchasers in the fume-free development.

52. Three people saw the significance of this so-called fourth rule independently: James R. Atwood, *see* Note, *An Economic Analysis of Land Use Conflicts,* 21 STAN. L. REV. 293, 315 (1969); my coauthor A. Douglas Melamed; and me. I have tried to find what, if anything, we had in common, and came up with one thing: At Yale College we had at different times each studied with Charles Edward Lindblom, a remarkable economist who was known for urging economists to be less model-building theorists and more concerned with facts on a case-by-case basis. In a way, as lawyers all three of us did what Lindblom urged economists to do, but in reverse. We examined legal case-by-case analysis in the light of a simple model.

53. *See* Calabresi, *supra* note 18.

2

Of Merit Goods

1. Richard A. Musgrave, The Theory of Public Finance: A Study in Public Economy (1959); James Tobin, *On Limiting the Domain of Inequality,* 13 J.L. & Econ. 263 (1970).

2. *See* Musgrave, *supra* note 1, at 13–15; Tobin, *supra* note 1, at 266–67.

3. R. H. Coase, *The Problem of Social Cost,* 3 J.L. & Econ. 1 (1960). What may not be noticed as much is the fact that societies also choose to use *command* to reduce or eliminate such externalities.

4. *But see infra* Chapter 4, Section A (discussing the role of comparative advantage in determining what in any society are in fact deemed merit goods).

5. *See* Margaret Jane Radin, Contested Commodities (1996).

6. Robert Bork, *Neutral Principles and Some First Amendment Problems,* 47 Indiana L.J. 1, 9–11 (1971).

7. *See* John Stuart Mill, *On Liberty, in* On Liberty and Other Essays 5, 93–103 (John Gray ed., Oxford Univ. Press 1991) (1859).

8. *See infra* Chapter 7, Sections A, B (showing that economists often ignore certain moral costs); *cf.* Guido Calabresi, Ideals, Beliefs, Attitudes, and the Law: Private Law Perspectives on a Public Law Problem 69–86 (1985) (exploring why tort law traditionally does not compensate for emotional damages).

9. *See infra* Chapter 7, Section C.

10. This does not mean that some internalization of these kinds of moral externalities does not happen. Charitable giving can be seen as seeking to bring about a private internalization of moral costs. *See infra* Chapter 3, note 20; *infra* Chapter 4, notes 13–14 and accompanying text.

11. Economists have traditionally had difficulty analyzing interdependent utility functions, that is, utility functions in which one person's utility depends on the utility (or other characteristics) of another person. Economic models generally assume simple wealth maximization, not altruism or vindictiveness. However, some economists have incorporated interdependent utility functions into their models. *See, e.g.,* A. Chakraborty, A. Citanna, & M. Ostrovsky, *Two-Sided Matching with Interdependent Values,* 145 J. Econ. Theory 85 (2010); Theodore C. Bergstrom, *Systems of Benevolent Utility Functions,* 1 J. Pub. Econ. Theory 71 (1999); Albert L. Danielsen, *Interdependent Utilities, Charity, and Pareto Optimality: Comment,* 89 Q. J. Econ. 477 (1975); George Daly & J. Fred Giertz, *Benevolence, Malevolence and Economic Theory,* 13 Pub. Choice 1 (1972); Lawrence D. Schall, *Interdependent Utilities*

and Pareto Optimality, 86 Q. J. Econ. 19 (1972); Kenneth E. Boulding, *Notes on a Theory of Philanthropy, in* Philanthropy and Public Policy (Frank G. Dickinson ed., 1962).

12. Of course we could solve this problem by equalizing the prevailing wealth distribution in society, so that everyone would have access to such merit goods on equal terms. However, we seemingly are not willing to do that, probably because we deem an unequal wealth distribution to be necessary to provide incentives for productive activity. *See infra* Chapter 3, Section A, Chapter 4, Section A.

13. *See, e.g.,* Cass R. Sunstein, Valuing Life: Humanizing the Regulatory State (2014); W. Kip Viscusi, *The Benefits of Mortality Risk Reduction: Happiness Surveys Versus the Value of a Statistical Life,* 62 Duke L.J. 1735 (2013); Thomas J. Kniesner, W. Kip Viscusi, Christopher Woock, & James P. Ziliak, *The Value of Statistical Life: Evidence from Panel Data,* 94 Rev. Econ. & Statistics 74 (2012); W. Kip Viscusi, *How to Value a Life,* 32 J. Econ. & Finance 311 (2008).

14. Guido Calabresi, *The Decision for Accidents: An Approach to No-Fault Allocation of Costs,* 78 Harv. L. Rev. 713 (1965).

15. *See New Attitudes on Auto Safety,* N.Y. Times, May 1, 1966, at 21.

16. *See* Guido Calabresi & Philip Bobbitt, Tragic Choices 39–42 (1978).

17. Apart from the difficulty of valuing things like life in the first place, there is also the problem that the price will not be constant. If you offer me $1,000 for a 1/1000 chance of my death I may take it, but if you offer me $500,000 for a ½ chance of my death I may throw you out the window. *See id.* at 116–17. I owe this insight to a comment Bruce Ackerman made as a law student attending my torts class (in which he was not enrolled).

18. Even life can be traded off against other values, such as equality. In the Supreme Court case *Cooper v. Aaron,* Solicitor General J. Lee Rankin argued that the deterioration of education in southern states, and political violence by governments resisting desegregation orders, should not overcome the constitutional requirement of equality—that the value of equality was, in this case, more important than life itself. Oral Argument, Day 1, Part 2 at 60:47 & Day 2, Part 3, at 2:50, Cooper v. Aaron, 358 U.S. 1 (No. 1), *available at* http://www.oyez.org/cases/1950-1959/1958/1958_1.

19. Calabresi & Bobbitt, *supra* note 16, at 40–41.

20. Oral Argument at 74:05, New York Times v. United States, 403 U.S. 17 (No. 1873), *available at* http://www.oyez.org/cases/1970-1979/1970/1970_1873. In his opinion, Justice Stewart noted that this hypothetical did not apply to the case at bar. *See* New York Times v. United States, 403 U.S. 713, 730 (1971)

(Stewart, J., concurring) ("I cannot say that disclosure of any of them will surely result in direct, immediate, and irreparable damage to our Nation or its people.").

21. This phenomenon bears a similarity to the endowment effect that has been central to behavioral economics. *See* Richard Thaler, *Toward a Positive Theory of Consumer Choice,* 1 J. ECON. BEHAVIOR & ORG. 39 (1980). Just as people place a higher value on things that they already own than on equivalent things that they do not yet own, they may place a higher value on safety that the government has already guaranteed than on safety that the government might guarantee in the future.

22. Generally tort law does so by combining liability rules with more stringent prohibitions on harmful conduct. *See infra* Chapter 6, Sections B, C. For example, we allow people to drive so long as they are willing and able to pay for the risk of accidents (by requiring them to buy automobile insurance and subjecting them to tort suits for accidents), but we also prohibit people from driving if they are below a certain age, fail to pass a license test, or drive under the influence of alcohol. Thus we use the market approach as a default to allocate automobile-related risk, but add on various command-based prohibitions that entirely exclude certain especially risky categories of driver (the young, the drunk, and those who cannot pass the relatively perfunctory licensing test). This heterodox approach reduces both commodification costs (by excluding some risky drivers that the market would include) and commandification costs (by relying mainly on the market to determine who can drive).

23. *See, e.g.,* Jules Coleman, *Corrective Justice and Wrongful Gain,* 11 J. LEGAL STUD. 421 (1982); John C. P. Goldberg & Benjamin C. Zipursky, *Torts as Wrongs,* 88 TEX. L. REV. 917 (2010).

24. *See, e.g.,* Richard L. Abel, *A Critique of Torts,* 37 UCLA L. REV. 785, 804–6 (1990) (criticizing tort damages as commodifying human experience).

25. This is so because the tort system compensates victims for, among other things, the future income they will lose owing to the tort in question. If victim *A* has twice the earning power of victim *B,* then, all else being equal, victim *A* will recover twice as much as victim *B* in compensatory damages stemming from lost future income.

26. *See, e.g.,* Abel, *supra* note 24, at 798–806 (arguing that unequal compensation in tort law reproduces and intensifies existing social inequalities); Leslie Bender, *Overview of Feminist Torts Scholarship,* 78 CORNELL L. REV. 575, 585–86 (arguing that tort law undercompensates women because damage calculations underestimate women's earning power in the market).

27. These alternatives could include a first-party insurance system in which people are required to insure themselves, or a government-run no-fault insurance system (such as exists in New Zealand) in which taxpayers and employers pay into a fund that compensates injury claimants without litigation. But of course our current system has many people who live off of it and defend it. The trial lawyers and defense research institute lawyers have interests as well, and it could be that one justification for our current tort litigation-based system is as a source of income for them, one which they, rationally from their point of view, fiercely and effectively defend. *See* Guido Calabresi, *The New Economic Analysis of Law: Scholarship, Sophistry, or Self-Indulgence?,* 68 Proc. Brit. Acad. 85, 97–98 (1982).

28. *See infra* Chapter 6.

29. *See, e.g.,* Riegel v. Medtronic, Inc., 552 U.S. 312 (2008) (holding that state common law tort claims concerning the safety of medical devices are preempted by FDA regulation); Press Release, Pharmaceutical Research and Manufacturers of America Statement on Federal Preemption, June 11, 2008.

30. *See* Peter H. Schuck, *FDA Preemption of State Tort Law in Drug Regulation: Finding the Sweet Spot,* 13 Roger Williams U. L. Rev. 73 (2008).

31. Guido Calabresi, *Remarks of Hon. Guido Calabresi,* 65 N.Y.U. Ann. Surv. Am. Law 435 (2010) (arguing that preemption decisions implicate the question of whether national, centralized decision making or local, diffuse decision making better allocates the cost of accidents); *see also infra* Chapter 6, Section B.

32. That is, we must consider not just the moral costs of using command versus torts to allocate harm, but also the administrative costs of running the tort system, and whether it is cheaper or more expensive than a command-based approach.

33. *See, e.g.,* Wyeth v. Levine, 555 U.S. 555 (2009) (holding that a woman who lost her hand to gangrene after injecting nausea medication could sue in tort in Vermont for inadequate labeling); Silkwood v. Kerr-McGee Corp., 464 U.S. 238, 251, 256 (1984) (in a lawsuit concerning radiation injuries at a nuclear power plant, stating that it is difficult to believe Congress would, without comment, remove all recourse for people harmed by such conduct).

34. *See* sources cited *supra* note 13; Shari Seidman Diamond, Michael J. Saks, & Stephan Landsman, *Juror Judgments About Liability and Damages: Sources of Variability and Ways to Increase Consistency,* 48 DePaul L. Rev. 301 (1998) (arguing that juries should be informed of the size of damages awarded in comparable prior cases).

35. Before one concludes, as a scholar, that the distributional concerns of pharmaceutical companies are unimportant, one must have a scholarly

reason for doing so. Simply to assert that they are unimportant is covertly to import one's own values into the analysis. *See* Calabresi, *supra* note 27, at 97–98. And it may also be the case that commandification of pharmaceutical regulation through national preemption is a better, cheaper, more efficient approach, all things considered. *See* Calabresi, *supra* note 31 (discussing the questions that must be asked in deciding whether to use regulation-based preemption).

3
Of Merit Goods and Inequality

1. At the same time, the fact that the United States has many people in jail—indeed, many more than any other country—suggests that incentives may often be negative. In any event, it is quite clear that the extensive use of incarceration likewise generates great inequality. *See, e.g.,* MICHELLE ALEXANDER, THE NEW JIM CROW: MASS INCARCERATION IN THE AGE OF COLORBLINDNESS (2013); BRUCE WESTERN, PUNISHMENT AND INEQUALITY IN AMERICA (2006).

2. *See* Michael H. Shapiro, *Who Merits Merit? Problems in Distributive Justice and Utility Posed by the New Biology,* 48 S. CAL. L. REV. 318 (1974) (describing "resource attractors" as "merit attributes" in the context of distributive justice claims); *see also* Marjorie E. Kornhauser, *The Morality of Money: American Attitudes Toward Wealth and the Income Tax,* 70 IND. L.J. 119 (1994) (reading Americans' ambivalence toward wealth in tax laws); Marjorie E. Kornhauser, *Equality, Liberty, and a Fair Income Tax,* 23 FORDHAM URB. L.J. 607 (1996) (describing intertwined accumulation and egalitarian strands of "moral economic individualism").

3. Ever since Coase, we know that external costs tend to get reduced, that if there are external costs, people often act to reduce them by paying those whose activities impose these costs to refrain from the activities in question. We are less likely to conceive in Coasean terms of internalizing externalities through command. Yet, whether we conceive of it in Coasean terms or not, the reduction of such costs occurs through both markets and command. And we should expect the same tendency to hold for the external *moral* costs being discussed here. In other words, one way that people may work to reduce moral costs is by command, by prohibiting the offending activities. Another way is through market-like altruistic behavior—for example, if it offends me that you sell your kidney, I may pay you not to do so. There is nothing in theory that prevents our attempting to reduce external moral costs in one

way or the other. Of course, in the case of selling body parts, it is unlikely that we can achieve the kind of market internalization that happens in other cases. But even where some market internalization is achievable, we may well supplement it with some internalization through command.

4. Many have argued, for instance, in favor of a market in transplantable organs, and such a market may have many virtues, including the creation of incentives to increase the available supply of organs. *See, e.g.,* Lloyd R. Cohen, *Increasing the Supply of Transplant Organs: The Virtues of a Futures Market,* 58 GEO. WASH. L. REV. 1 (1989); Jesse Dukeminier, Jr., *Supplying Organs for Transplantation,* 68 MICH. L. REV. 811 (1970) (suggesting several alternatives to direct sale, and arguing that some form of remuneration may be necessary to increase supply). Yet there may be deeper difficulties with establishing markets in cases involving organs or life-saving technologies. *See infra* note 36; *see also* I. Glenn Cohen, *Regulating the Organ Market: Normative Foundations for Market Regulation,* 77 LAW & CONTEMP. PROBS. 71 (2014) (mapping the arguments against a free market in organs onto the various mechanisms of regulation that each argument would justify).

5. RICHARD A. MUSGRAVE, THE THEORY OF PUBLIC FINANCE: A STUDY IN PUBLIC ECONOMY 13–14 (1959); Richard A. Musgrave, *Merit Goods, in* 3 THE NEW PALGRAVE: A DICTIONARY OF ECONOMICS 452 (John Eatwell et al. eds., 1987) (including health care as an example of merit goods); Edward D. Burmeister, Jr., Note, *Cost-Benefit Analysis and the National Environmental Policy Act of 1969,* 24 STAN. L. REV. 1092, 1108 (1972) ("The argument that the political process is the appropriate mode of decisionmaking thus asserts that environmental quality is a merit good—that values of environmental amenities should be determined on an equalitarian basis, with consideration of tradeoffs between environmental quality and other merit goods, and from a perspective of social concern rather than of private self-interest."); Steven J. Eagle, *Environmental Amenities, Private Property, and Public Policy,* 44 NAT. RESOURCES J. 425, 436 (2004) ("A problem related to the valuation of environmental amenities is their asserted status as 'merit goods.'"); *see also* Endre Stavang, *Tolerance Limits and Temporal Priority in Environmental Civil Liability,* 17 INT'L REV. L. & ECON. 553 (1997); Endre Stavang, *Property in Emissions: Analysis of the Norwegian GHG ETS with References also to the UK and the EU,* 17 ENVTL. L. & MGMT. 209 (2005) (emphasizing the fundamental importance of environmental goods).

6. During the Civil War, draftees were allowed at first to purchase a substitute, but because of the administrative complexity, which led to a lucrative arbitrage in military service, this system was replaced by one that permitted draftees to pay a simple fee to be exempt. *See* GUIDO CALABRESI & PHILIP BOBBITT, TRAGIC CHOICES 159–60 (1978).

7. *See* Moore v. Regents of Univ. of California, 51 Cal. 3d 120, 177 (1990) (noting that the sale of blood and plasma "in nonvital amounts" is permissible and that, to avoid products liability laws, such transactions are typically characterized by state law as the sale of services). There is also the celebrated debate between Richard Titmuss and Kenneth Arrow over whether blood ought to be commodified and sold, or should be supplied only through altruistic donations. *See* RICHARD M. TITMUSS, THE GIFT RELATIONSHIP: FROM HUMAN BLOOD TO SOCIAL POLICY (1970) (arguing against the commodification of blood); Kenneth J. Arrow, *Gifts and Exchanges*, 1 PHIL. & PUB. AFF. 343 (1972) (arguing in favor). *See also* Firat Bilgel & Brian Galle, *Paying for Altruism: The Case of Organ Donation Revisited* (Boston College Legal Studies Research Paper No. 337, Sept. 2014) (using data from tax incentive legislation passed in New York to show that kidney donation rates rose in response to financial incentives).

8. *See* Lloyd R. Cohen, *supra* note 4, at 1 n.1 (citing several sources that argue for the use of market incentives to increase the supply of transplantable organs).

9. For an account of political contributions as merit goods, see my concurring opinion in Ognibene v. Parkes, 671 F.3d 174, 197 (2d Cir. 2011) (Calabresi, J., concurring). *See also* Barack H. Obama, President of the United States, Remarks by the President in State of the Union Address (Jan. 27, 2010), http://www.whitehouse.gov/the-press-office/remarks-president-state-union-address ("With all due deference to separation of powers, last week the Supreme Court reversed a century of law that I believe will open the floodgates for special interests—including foreign corporations—to spend without limit in our elections. I don't think American elections should be bankrolled by America's most powerful interests, or worse, by foreign entities. They should be decided by the American people. And I'd urge Democrats and Republicans to pass a bill that helps to correct some of these problems.").

10. As already mentioned, *see supra* note 6, the first draft system implemented during the Civil War, a system that allowed draftees to purchase a substitute, was subsequently replaced by a buyout provision that required payment of a simple fee to be exempt from service. A volunteer army differs from a draft with a buyout provision in either of these two forms in being slightly more wealth distribution–neutral because of the relative progressivity of giving a benefit (payment for service) as compared with imposing a cost (payment to be exempt from service). In other words, a volunteer army confers on everyone a right that can be sold, and the additional payment is incrementally more valuable to the poor, whereas a draft with a buyout (whether in the form of payment of a flat fee or purchase of a direct substitute) imposes a cost, which

will be experienced by the poor as incrementally more burdensome. But all are crucially affected by the existing distribution of wealth.

11. Chief Justice Roberts has quipped, " 'Leveling the playing field' can sound like a good thing. But in a democracy, campaigning for office is not a game. It is a critically important form of speech." *Arizona Free Enter. Club's Freedom Club PAC v. Bennett,* 131 S. Cᴛ. 2806, 2826 (2011). Wordplay not-withstanding, the reason that leveling the playing field may well be of critical importance in a democracy is that unlimited campaign contributions may permit the rich to drown out the poor and, indeed, may deprive the poor of a fundamental aspect of their speech rights—namely, the ability effectively to register the intensity of their political beliefs. *See* Ognibene v. Parkes, 671 F.3d 174, 198 (2d Cir. 2011) (Calabresi, J., concurring).

12. *See* Kᴇɴɴᴇᴛʜ E. Bᴏᴜʟᴅɪɴɢ, Tʜᴇ Mᴇᴀɴɪɴɢ ᴏꜰ ᴛʜᴇ Tᴡᴇɴᴛɪᴇᴛʜ Cᴇɴᴛᴜʀʏ 135–36 (1964).

13. With respect to child rights and drafts, for example, markets would not be inherently problematic for the second-order determination as to who should procreate or serve in the military, were it not for the differential ability of the wealthy to have (or avoid) the good (or bad). Hence, a wealth-neutral market for the second-order decision may permit individuals to express a preference without imposing the moral externalities associated with the distribution of wealth more generally. Yet whether markets, even wealth-neutral ones, may function as well for the first-order determination as to how much of the good (or bad) to produce is a different question. Although the two determinations often affect one another, they are still separate, and what is desirable in making the second-order determination may not be so when it comes to the first-order determination. *See, e.g.,* Cᴀʟᴀʙʀᴇsɪ & Bᴏʙʙɪᴛᴛ, *supra* note 6, at 87–89 (noting important distinctions and interactions between the first- and second-order determinations).

14. *Cf.* Robert Burt, *Why We Should Keep Prisoners from the Doctors: Reflections on the Detroit Psychosurgery Case,* 5 Hᴀsᴛɪɴɢs Cᴇɴᴛᴇʀ Rᴇᴘᴏʀᴛ 25 (1974) (weighing possible benefits to prisoners of voluntary psychosurgery against costs to society, and concluding that not permitting such surgery is ultimately justified by the latter costs).

15. Gregory Keating, for one, has taken the Rawlsian conception of autonomy from liberal political theory to explain a variety of issues in tort law. *See, e.g.,* Gregory C. Keating, *Rawlsian Fairness and Regime Choice in the Law of Accidents,* 72 Fᴏʀᴅʜᴀᴍ L. Rᴇᴠ. 1857, 1921 (2004); Gregory C. Keating, *Reasonableness and Rationality in Negligence Theory,* 48 Sᴛᴀɴ. L. Rᴇᴠ. 311, 384 (1996); Gregory Keating, *Strict Liability Wrongs, in* Pʜɪʟᴏsᴏᴘʜɪᴄᴀʟ Fᴏᴜɴᴅᴀ-ᴛɪᴏɴs ᴏꜰ ᴛʜᴇ Lᴀᴡ ᴏꜰ Tᴏʀᴛs 292 (John Oberdiek ed., 2014).

16. *See, e.g.,* JEREMY BENTHAM, *Anarchical Fallacies, in* 2 THE WORKS OF JEREMY BENTHAM 489, 501 (John Bowring ed., 1843) (describing the doctrine of natural rights as "simple nonsense," and that of "natural and imprescriptible rights" as "nonsense upon stilts").

17. *Cf., e.g.,* Burt, *supra* note 14 (arguing that the moral costs to society of allowing prisoners to consent to psychosurgery may justify a total prohibition, even where such surgery may well confer significant benefits on the individual prisoners). *But cf.* Louis Kaplow & Steven Shavell, *Why the Legal System Is Less Efficient than the Income Tax in Redistributing Income,* 23 J. LEGAL STUD. 667 (1994) (arguing that legal rules with worrisome distributional effects are better accommodated by redistributing wealth via tax and transfer than by using inefficient legal rules to distribute goods to the poor in the first instance).

18. Even under conditions of almost absolute egalitarianism or wealth neutrality, we may well feel that one must still be given a certain education and a certain sphere of bodily integrity, however minimal, and that these should be inalienable, that one should not be able to forgo them, for example, by selling oneself into slavery. *Cf.* BRUCE A. ACKERMAN, SOCIAL JUSTICE IN THE LIBERAL STATE 3–192 (1980) (arguing for a conception of "undominated equality" as a condition of market freedom that would include the right to receive, *inter alia,* a liberal education and a fair share of economic power); Martha C. Nussbaum, *Foreword: Constitutions and Capabilities: "Perception" Against Lofty Formalism,* 121 HARV. L. REV. 4, 15 n.15 (2007) (listing essential human capabilities that correspond to basic entitlements or human rights, some of which are enshrined as constitutional guarantees, and including in that list both adequate education and bodily integrity); Areto A. Imoukhuede, *Education Rights and the New Due Process,* 47 IND. L. REV. 467 (2014) (arguing that the provision of a quality education is essential to human dignity and democracy).

19. By definition, a Pareto superior move leaves everyone as well off as before and makes at least one person better off. This means, then, that no one is harmed, and if someone is morally injured by a transaction between two willing participants, that third party *is harmed.* Indeed, if such a move were truly Paretian and injured nobody, it *would* be permitted. *Cf.* Guido Calabresi, *The Pointlessness of Pareto: Carrying Coase Further,* 100 YALE L.J. 1211 (1991).

20. Again, people will often act to reduce external moral costs, and such costs can be internalized in different ways, by quasi-market means like charity or by command. As to certain goods like basic education, the moral costs of having their allocation depend on the prevailing distribution of wealth may be

so substantial as to necessitate straight command and straight equality. As to others, like top-flight education, the existence of numerous market interventions, such as scholarships or financial aid, may suffice to reduce the moral costs to tolerable levels. *See infra* Chapter 4, note 13. Even in the allocation of body parts, one can see versions of this tendency to reduce moral externalities. For example, when the news media cover a story of someone who is unable to pay for a lifesaving operation, people often donate large amounts of money in an attempt to diminish, by means of individual gift, the moral costs of our allocating lifesaving surgery in visibly wealth-dependent ways.

21. *See* Kaplow & Shavell, *supra* note 17.

22. In criticizing Titmuss with respect to allocation of blood, Arrow points out that possible alternatives to pure markets include not only altruistic giving, but also "authority and hierarchy," as well as "rational bureaucracy with place determined by merit." Arrow, *supra* note 7, at 346. Each such alternative, whether quasi-market, pure command, or quasi-command, may give rise to externalities of different sorts with respect to the allocation of different goods.

23. *See* Calabresi & Bobbitt, *supra* note 6, at 49–50, 143–46 (summarizing the virtues and vices of different allocative methods); *id.* at 195–97 (describing movement of society among different methods over time in response to the perceived defects of the preexisting method).

24. *See infra* Chapter 5, Section B.

25. Following Coase, several economists have examined the distinction between centralized governmental command structures and private decentralized ones, such as the firm, as well as the relative advantages of each. *See, e.g.,* Oliver E. Williamson, *Markets and Hierarchies: Some Elementary Considerations,* 63 Am. Econ. Rev. 316 (1973); Armen A. Alchian & Harold Demsetz, *Production, Information Costs, and Economic Organization,* 62 Am. Econ. Rev. 777 (1972); Sanford J. Grossman & Oliver D. Hart, *The Costs and Benefits of Ownership: A Theory of Vertical and Lateral Integration,* 94 J. Pol. Econ. 691 (1986); Oliver Hart & John Moore, *Property Rights and the Nature of the Firm,* 98 J. Pol. Econ. 1119 (1990).

26. *See* Calabresi & Bobbitt, *supra* note 6, at 162–65.

27. In contrast to wealth, which tends to be distributed similarly across levels, power can vary widely at different levels: local, state, and national. For that reason, command can be structured in any number of complicated ways, and this fact about command may make its use more flexible than the use of markets. My own deferment, as I say, was made possible no doubt by the relative local significance of my being Italian American, a significance that was likely absent at the national and the state level. To take another example, Morris Tyler, who was the great-great-grandfather of my wife, Anne, was

voted out of office as mayor of New Haven after he read the Riot Act to the draft rioters—assertedly, predominantly Irish immigrants who had fled the Great Famine and who, having no involvement with slavery and the issues attached to it, did not wish to serve in the Union Army. *See* IVER BERNSTEIN, THE NEW YORK CITY DRAFT RIOTS: THEIR SIGNIFICANCE FOR AMERICAN SOCIETY AND POLITICS IN THE AGE OF THE CIVIL WAR (1990). The extreme unpopularity of the draft was local. The state had a different ethnic mix, which took a different view of the importance of abolishing slavery and saving the Union, and Tyler was soon elected lieutenant governor of Connecticut.

28. *See* CALABRESI & BOBBITT, *supra* note 6, at 92–103; *see also id.* at 54, 92, 122–24 (noting that, where modified and nonmoney markets are used for specific goods, there is inevitably an incentive for corruption, since those who have more money or power or time will use what they have an excess of to obtain for themselves the scarce good that is supposed to be allocated on another basis).

29. Command was present in the decision both to ration some goods and to institute direct controls on the price of other goods in order to prevent inflation. The U.S. government's stated reasons for rationing items like sugar, butter, and meat during World War II were that these items were in short supply and that rationing was the only way to ensure that everyone got a fair share. *See, e.g.,* AMY BENTLEY, EATING FOR VICTORY: FOOD RATIONING AND THE POLITICS OF DOMESTICITY 1 (1998) ("This is your Government's guarantee of your fair share of goods made scarce by war." [quoting War Ration Book No. 2]). Price controls depended on rationing to succeed, but they also worked in part because people were not pressured to buy, given the widely held conviction that the war mobilization effort, which brought high employment and a systemic disequilibrium between demand and supply, was simply "an interlude between depressions." JOHN KENNETH GALBRAITH, A THEORY OF PRICE CONTROL 37 (1952). The *inequality* reason was at work as well, however, and the idea was very much present that both rich and poor would bear a fair share of the burdens of war and that the state would work to protect all, but especially the most vulnerable, from unduly suffering the costs of war. *Cf. Text of Prime Minister Churchill's Report to Parliament on the Progress of the War,* N.Y. TIMES, Oct. 9, 1940, at 4 (outlining a scheme of social insurance for bombed buildings and of broader community and state support for delivering food and shelter to those affected).

30. *See* CALABRESI & BOBBITT, *supra* note 6, at 19 (defining first-order and second-order determinations).

31. One might argue, however, that an advantage of a market-based decision as to how many soldiers will become available at what cost is that it

would give us information as to the desirability of the particular war as seen by the populace at large rather than simply the collective decision makers. In other words, a market determination of the first-order decision gives a decentralized and broadly based view of the desirability of the particular good or bad, and *that,* one might argue, may be useful with respect to armies no less than with respect to other goods. *Cf.* Bernard Rostker, America Goes to War: Managing the Force During Times of Stress and Uncertainty 5 (noting that prior to World War I, the British army was voluntary and that its size was treated as a constraint on foreign policy rather than as a factor that could be adjusted by command through a draft); Beth Bailey, America's Army: Making the All-Volunteer Force (2009) (describing arguments about the merits of markets in military service in the post–Vietnam War transition to an all-volunteer force).

32. Again, the existence of moral costs means that a decision to modify the market in this way does not violate Pareto. As I have elsewhere argued, if we *could* reduce these costs in some other way that satisfies Pareto, we *would.* *See* Calabresi, *supra* note 19.

33. *See* Calabresi & Bobbitt, *supra* note 6, at 92–117.

34. At some level, any good is an alternative to any other good. But some goods are closer alternatives than others. To the extent that people would prefer to trade off goods that are outside the rationing scheme for goods within the scheme, the rationing scheme harms individual desires.

35. *But see supra* note 31.

36. On the other hand it may be very difficult to have a wealth distribution–neutral market in body parts that are necessary to keep one alive, such as hearts, lungs, etc. With a wealth distribution–dependent market in such organs, the market clears because the rich simply outbid the poor and get the organs. But if everyone had the same bidding power they would engage in "desperation bidding," so both the poor and the rich would put in all of their wealth because they all want so badly to live. *See* Calabresi & Bobbitt, *supra* note 6, at 117. If the demand for a good is extraordinarily inelastic, then a wealth distribution–neutral market will feature people bidding up without limit. And because there is not enough to go around, the market will not clear. That would not happen if the high bids increased the supply sufficiently, or the high prices made people decide to do without the good. But when life is at stake on both the supply and the demand side it is hard to imagine those things happening. The supply of available kidneys could probably be increased by letting people bid up the price through a market. But with hearts the matter is much more difficult, unless, for example, the high prices led to research that resulted in hearts from cadavers becoming usable.

37. Similarly, the total amount that one may contribute to political campaigns, as well as in what ways one may contribute, may or may not be something that a society wishes to decide collectively. In either case, the issue of whether individuals' decisions regarding political contributions should be relatively independent of wealth is different and separate from the issue of whether the *total* contributed should be determined collectively or by individual desire expressed in the market.

38. *But see supra* note 31.

39. The analogy of non-military service to compulsory education is not meant to imply that education itself isn't *also* a merit good. The decision that a certain good (or bad) should be distributed by straight command and imposed on all equally is not the same as the decision that its allocation should not depend on the prevailing distribution of wealth.

40. The moral costs of having military service depend on wealth do not necessarily attach to other inegalitarian allocative methods, for example, those that use such conventionally accepted standards for exemption as age and health. *Cf.* CALABRESI & BOBBITT, *supra* note 6, at 37.

41. To take only two examples, bribery, which is an instance of the wealthy acquiring (through money) power that they do not otherwise directly possess, is very difficult to catch without also instituting extensive auditing and accounting requirements, all of which are costly. Likewise, to catch the cop on the beat who takes an apple from the fruit stand—and who thereby adds to his wealth by using the power that he *does* have to acquire goods that he has not paid for and may be unwilling to buy, given his salary—would impose exorbitant monitoring costs.

4
Of Merit Goods Generally

1. *See* Louis Kaplow & Steven Shavell, *Why the Legal System Is Less Efficient than the Income Tax in Redistributing Income,* 23 J. LEGAL STUD. 667 (1994) (arguing that redistribution through the income tax system is superior to redistribution through legal rules such as tort liability). For criticism of this argument, see, e.g., Ronen Avraham et al., *Revisiting the Roles of Legal Rules and Tax Rules in Income Redistribution: A Response to Kaplow & Shavell,* 89 IOWA L. REV. 1125 (2004); Zachary Liscow, Note, *Reducing Inequality on the Cheap: When Legal Rule Design Should Incorporate Equity as Well as Efficiency,* 123 YALE L.J. 2478 (2014); Chris Sanchirico, *Taxes Versus Legal Rules as Instruments for Equity: A More Equitable View,* 29 J. LEGAL STUD. 797 (2000); Lee Anne

Fennell & Richard H. McAdams, *The Distributive Deficit in Law and Economics* (Coase-Sandor Working Paper Series in Law and Economics No. 713, 2015). The idea that general income redistribution should take priority over particular allocations of goods or entitlements has also been prominently expressed by Milton Friedman. *See* Milton Friedman, Capitalism and Freedom 190–95 (1962).

2. *See, e.g.,* Louis Kaplow & Steven Shavell, Fairness Versus Welfare (2002).

3. But of course "equality" has many different possible meanings. *See* Amartya Sen, *Equality of What?, in* Equal Freedom: Selected Tanner Lectures on Human Values 307 (Stephen Darwall ed., 1995). And there are even some who find no value whatsoever in equality. *See* Friedrich A. Hayek, *The Atavism of Social Justice, in* New Studies in Philosophy, Politics, Economics and the History of Ideas (1978).

4. *See, e.g.,* Arthur Okun, Equality and Efficiency: The Big Trade Off (1975); Lee Anne Fennell & Richard H. McAdams, Fairness in Law and Economics (2013) (in particular Part II Section A, discussing trade-offs between fairness and efficiency). Indeed, even John Rawls has argued that inequality can produce incentives that benefit all in society. *See* John Rawls, A Theory of Justice 151, 158, 279 (1971).

5. But, again, "equality" in the distribution of a good has many possible meanings. It could mean equality in distribution of that good, equality of marginal utility from that good, equality of capability to enjoy that good, and so forth. *See* Sen, *supra* note 3.

6. There is an important difference between deciding how to allocate goods and bads in a particular case, and deciding how to allocate them in general. A rule that seems morally right for a particular set of circumstances may not work if it is imposed on society as a whole. For instance, a jury that is presented with a particular case where a person has been wronged, and is asked whether or not to award that person significant damages, might choose to do so. But that same jury, if it were asked whether in general people who have suffered this kind of wrong should be awarded damages in that amount, might make an entirely different decision. *See* Guido Calabresi & Philip Bobbitt, Tragic Choices 57–64 (1978).

7. *See supra* Chapter 3, note 29.

8. *See* Okun, *supra* note 4.

9. *See* Friedman, *supra* note 1; Kaplow & Shavell, *supra* note 1. But such an assertion ignores the nature of people's actual tastes and values. Some people care much more about the allocation of particular goods than about general equality.

10. The treatment of wealth distribution–based externalities is, in this respect, different from the treatment of classic externalities. For classic externalities—those that derive from actions that impose costs on third parties (like polluting) or confer benefits on third parties (like vaccination)—we sometimes control the actions through command and other nonmarket mechanisms so as to increase or decrease the externality directly, and do so regardless of the market's dependence on wealth inequalities. By contrast, when we remove wealth distribution–based externalities from the market, we do so precisely because we are offended to see goods and bads conferred on the basis of wealth. We do this because it is that wealth dependence that causes the externality. It also bears noting that the same problem that exists for goods that are distributed by relative wealth in a market-based system also exists for goods that are distributed by relative power in a command-based system. If goods and bads are distributed through command, those with access to political power will receive more goods and fewer bads. We might remedy this by distributing power more equally, but that decreases the incentive for people to obtain power. Or we might instead take the particular good out of a command-based distribution and distribute it by lottery, market, or some other mechanism.

11. *See* Terry M. Moe, *Beyond the Free Market: The Structure of School Choice,* 2008 B.Y.U. L. Rev. 557, 561–64 ("Public school parents are [typically] not allowed to choose which public school their kids attend, but they are allowed to choose where their families will live. . . . Public schools are provided free of cost by the government. Parents can choose to send their kids to private schools, but private schools are costly.").

12. *See infra* Chapter 5.

13. Altruistically paying for other people's education through scholarships is also a Coasean method to reduce externalities caused by wealth dependence in the distribution of merit goods. If I give money for a scholarship for the poor, this helps internalize the negative externality by reducing the extent to which people are unhappy about unequal distribution of education. So charity may reduce this unhappiness by making the distribution of merit goods more equal, as well as satisfying people's taste and desire for altruism. The movement for "effective altruism" is motivated by this outcome-focused purpose of charity. *See* Peter Singer, The Most Good You Can Do: How Effective Altruism Is Changing Ideas About Living Ethically (2015).

14. There are a variety of different payment structures that can help make higher education more wealth distribution–neutral, and they can do so in different ways. Scholarships simply reduce the up-front cost of education, so that the less wealthy do not have to pay as much. Tuition postponement

loans allow students to reduce the up-front cost of education, and then to pay that cost in the future when they have high earnings (due in part to their education). Such loans can also be structured in such a way that the principal owed is reduced or even eliminated if the student does not earn very much money after entering the workforce.

15. For instance, arguments that charter schools are ineffective or harmful cohere with the distributional interests of teachers' unions, since charter schools are able to hire nonunion teachers in some states. *See* Matthew Kaminski, *Eva Moskowitz: Teachers Union Enemy No. 1,* WALL STREET JOURNAL, Feb. 16, 2014 ("[T]eachers unions and their political allies also treat charters as an existential threat. Charters hire teachers who don't have to join and pay union dues, and who work outside the traditional system."). And arguments for the effectiveness of vouchers and parochial schools align with the distributional interests of churches. *See* Al Baker, *Cardinal Dolan To Lobby for Tax Credit That Rewards Donations to Education,* N.Y. TIMES, Mar. 17, 2014.

16. Such modified market mechanisms for distributing access to schools also create externalities beyond their effects on education. For instance, in the South white parents have been able to use parochial and private schools to preserve segregation in education by sending their students to private schools that are predominantly white. Also, giving parochial schools access to publicly funded vouchers may be a creative way to finance intragroup altruism, since it funnels money to charitable institutions like churches that can then afford to do more (for instance, vouchers systems have helped to increase the compensation of nuns, who are often badly underpaid).

17. In light of Kaplow's and Shavell's argument that we should only pursue distributive goals by equalizing people's general income level, and not through particular entitlements, *see* Kaplow & Shavell, *supra* note 1, it would be interesting to know what they might say about our peculiar system of education, which has a variety of mechanisms to correct for unequal distribution of education, including some that operate through individual choices like scholarships, donations, etc.

18. For instance, health care for the elderly and for the poor has been largely taken out of the private market in the United States, and has been provided by the government for many decades through Medicare and Medicaid.

19. People's fear of the government making end-of-life-decisions that would affect them made the charge that the Affordable Care Act would institute "death panels" particularly politically effective. *See* Brendan Nyhan, *Why the "Death Panel" Myth Wouldn't Die: Misinformation in the Health Care Reform Debate,* 8 FORUM 1, 8–11 (2010).

20. *See* CALABRESI & BOBBITT, *supra* note 6, at 150–57.

21. *See supra* Chapter 3, note 36.

22. For instance, during World War II people were chosen for military duty according to their particular skills through a pure commandification system—a truly *selective* service. *See* LEWIS B. HERSHEY, OUTLINE OF HISTORICAL BACKGROUND OF SELECTIVE SERVICE AND CHRONOLOGY (1965); *see also* CALABRESI & BOBBITT, *supra* note 6, at 162.

23. The baseball player Joe DiMaggio, for example, served in the military in World War II, but did so as a physical education instructor in the United States. He did not see active combat. *See* Bart Barnes, *Joltin' Joe Has Gone Away,* WASH. POST, Mar. 8, 1999, at A1. This was a general pattern—famous actors, athletes, etc. often served in relatively safe roles during the war.

24. The Supreme Court has struck down laws that limit campaign expenditures on the ground that these laws restrict speech and benefit incumbents, notwithstanding the concern that such campaign expenditures are a source of corruption. *See* Citizens United v. Federal Election Commission, 558 U.S. 310 (2010). However, it has upheld limits on campaign contributions on the ground that such limits combat corruption, notwithstanding that they benefit incumbents and restrict speech. *See* Buckley v. Valeo, 424 U.S. 1 (1976). It is difficult to see how contributions are connected with corruption but expenditures are not.

25. *See, e.g.,* Gene Nichol, Citizens United *and the Roberts Court's War on Democracy,* 27 GA. ST. U. L. REV. 1007 (2011).

26. *See* Ognibene v. Parkes, 671 F.3d 174, 197–201 (2d Cir. 2011) (Calabresi, J., concurring); Landell v. Sorrell, 406 F.3d 159, 165 (2d Cir. 2005) (Calabresi, J., concurring in denial of rehearing en banc).

27. In this area, as in the areas of education and health care, allocational decisions impose several kinds of costs on people. One kind is purely moral costs, which are incurred because people object to the allocation that comes about. Another is purely nonmoral costs, such as the risk of contracting cancer or of losing economic resources. There are also mixed moral and nonmoral costs, such as where an unequal distribution of educational resources is both morally objectionable in itself and leads to worse lives for those at the bottom. My treatment of campaign regulation here focuses on moral costs, even though these may comprise only one category of costs resulting from uncontrolled campaign contributions.

28. When the Court acts in a countermajoritarian way, it imposes large costs on the majority, and so the Court had better be quite sure that the Constitution requires its action. *See* JOHN HART ELY, DEMOCRACY AND DISTRUST (1980) (arguing that countermajoritarian Supreme Court decisions are best justified where they preserve minority civil and political rights that

are unprotected by majoritarian processes); ALEXANDER BICKEL, THE LEAST DANGEROUS BRANCH: THE SUPREME COURT AT THE BAR OF POLITICS (1962) (exploring the tension between judicial review and democracy, and arguing for a restrained approach to judicial review).

29. *See* ELY, *supra* note 28; Guido Calabresi, *The Supreme Court, 1990 Term Foreword: Antidiscrimination and Constitutional Accountability (What the Bork–Brennan Debate Ignores),* 105 HARV. L. REV. 20 (1991).

30. *See, e.g.,* Reynolds v. Sims, 377 U.S. 533 (1964) (establishing the majoritarian constitutional principle that legislative districts should be equally sized to ensure all votes count roughly the same—the contrary antimajoritarian principle would be difficult to justify on antidiscrimination grounds); Calabresi, *supra* note 29, at 91–103 (describing a version of judicial review under which legislation can be permanently struck down only if it violates an antidiscrimination principle).

31. *See* Ognibene v. Parkes, 671 F.3d 174, 197–201 (2d Cir. 2011) (Calabresi, J., concurring) (advocating antidistortion measures that would ensure relatively equal access in political contributions regardless of wealth); Luke 21:1–4 ("As Jesus looked up, he saw the rich putting their gifts into the temple treasury. He also saw a poor widow put in two very small copper coins. 'Truly I tell you,' he said, 'this poor widow has put in more than all the others. All these people gave their gifts out of their wealth; but she out of her poverty put in all she had to live on.' ").

32. Some of these measures are likely to affect the capacity of people to express themselves through money, and some are likely to protect the power of incumbents. Thus some policies are more likely to run against what the Supreme Court has understandably been concerned about, while others are less so. For instance, a system in which every person has a hard and relatively low contribution limit would likely benefit incumbents, since there would be fewer available resources for challengers to overcome the built-in advantages of incumbents. And imposing a hard cap on campaign contributions or expenditures from the wealthy would restrict the ability of the wealthy to advocate their opinions. On the other hand, subsidizing campaign contributions and third-party expenditures might benefit low-name recognition challengers (assuming the benefits did not go disproportionately to incumbents), and might well increase (not restrain) election-related speech.

33. *See infra* Chapter 7.

34. People don't only bring in the government to reduce the moral costs from unequal distribution of merit goods; they also sometimes act in Coasean ways on their own to try to reduce these costs, for example, by financing educational scholarships. *See* discussion *supra* note 13.

5
Of Altruism, Beneficence, and Not-for-Profit Institutions

1. *See* Timothy Besley & Maitreesh Ghatak, *Retailing Public Goods: The Economics of Corporate Social Responsibility*, 91 J. Pub. Econ. 1645 (2007) (suggesting that for-profit firms might have a comparative advantage over governments in providing public goods); John L. Fizel & Thomas S. Nunnikhoven, *Technical Efficiency of For-Profit and Non-Profit Nursing Homes*, 13 Managerial & Decision Econ. 429 (1992) (finding results that support the hypothesis that for-profit nursing homes are more efficient than nonprofit ones); Carrie Lips, *"Edupreneurs:" A Survey of For-Profit Education*, Pol'y Analysis (Nov. 20, 2000) (arguing that for-profit education organizations are creative and cost-efficient). *But cf.* Edward L. Glaeser & Andrei Shleifer, *Not-for-Profit Entrepreneurs*, 82 J. Pub. Econ. 99 (2001) (arguing that the nonprofit form can protect parties from expropriation by the entrepreneur, and signal the entrepreneur's taste for producing high-quality products).

2. *See* Mark McClellan & Douglas Staiger, *Comparing Hospital Quality at For-Profit and Not-for-Profit Hospitals, in* The Changing Hospital Industry: Comparing For-Profit and Not-for-Profit Institutions 93 (David M. Cutler ed., 2000) (finding that nonprofits are slightly better at caring for certain kinds of patients than for-profits); Sang-Mok Kang & Moon-Hwee Kim, *The Cost Efficiency of Regional Public Hospitals in South Korea*, 5 Modern Econ. 989, 990 & n.3 (2014) (noting that public hospitals in Korea are less efficient than private hospitals, because the government imposes mandates on public hospitals); *see also supra* Chapter 3, note 7 (discussing the debate between Richard Titmuss and Kenneth Arrow over whether it is better to provide blood through altruistic donation or through a market).

3. There are, of course, economists who have looked at the questions involved in altruism and beneficence much more deeply. To name just a few, see, e.g., Kenneth Arrow, *supra* Chapter 3, note 7; George Daly & J. Fred Giertz, *Benevolence, Malevolence and Economic Theory*, 13 Pub. Choice 1 (1972); and especially, Kenneth E. Boulding, *Notes on a Theory of Philanthropy, in* Philanthropy and Public Policy (Frank G. Dickinson ed., 1962). There is, moreover, as Albert Hirschman has written, a much greater variety of mixed motivations for behavior than a simple "self-interest versus benevolence" dichotomy. For instance, people might engage in noninstrumental behavior with some instrumental motives in the background, or use an instrumental reason as one of many motivations for a particular action. *See* Albert O. Hirschman, *The Concept of Interest: From Euphemism to Tautology, in* Rival Views of Market Society and Other Recent Essays 52–53 (1986).

4. *See, e.g.,* James Andreoni, *Altruism and Donations to Public Goods: A Theory of Warm-Glow Giving,* 100 Econ. J. 464 (1990) (arguing that many donors to nonprofits act out of egoistic motivations); Hirschman, *supra* note 3, at 48–51 (detailing the efforts of nineteenth- and twentieth-century economists to define the entire range of human behavior as self-interested, thus expanding the concept of self-interest beyond recognition).

5. *See, e.g.,* George J. Stigler & Gary S. Becker, *De Gustibus Non Est Disputandum,* 67 Am. Econ. Rev. 76, 76 (1977) ("[O]ne does not argue over tastes for the same reason that one does not argue over the Rocky Mountains—both are there, will be there next year, too, and are the same to all men.").

6. Roland McKean, *The Economics of Trust, Altruism and Corporate Responsibility, in* Altruism, Morality, and Economic Theory 29, 30 (Edmund S. Phelps ed., 1975). The point has also been made in poetry (as indicated to me by Robert Cooter). *See* William Butler Yeats, *For Anne Gregory, in* The Winding Stair and Other Poems (1933).

7. Indeed, persuasion of this sort can be used as either a command tool or as a market tool to get others to behave in more desired ways. Institutions like compulsory schooling, mandatory training programs, and so forth all seek to achieve certain behavior not by commanding such behavior directly, but by persuading people to adopt it. On the other hand, persuasion is also a tool of the market. Advertisers, educational service providers, media companies, law firms, and other major sectors of the private economy provide persuasive services designed to promote certain behavior. *See* Deirdre N. McCloskey, Knowledge and Persuasion in Economics 76–84 (1994).

8. For example, in Italy the introduction of a law rewarding people for donating blood with a paid day off from work led to a 40 percent increase in blood donations. This is a clever mechanism to reward people for blood donations without creating a private market in blood. *See* Nicola Lacetera, Mario Macis, & Robert Slonim, *Economic Rewards to Motivate Blood Donations,* 340 Science 927, 927 (2013). Further, the use of tax incentives to encourage charitable giving can lead to a sustained culture of giving that persists even if the tax incentives are taken away. *See* Melissa Leong, *Budget Aims to Get First-Time Charitable Donors on Board,* Fin. Post, Mar. 23, 2013 (describing a federal tax policy in Canada that gives first-time donors a one-off 25 percent charitable tax credit for donations up to one thousand dollars, with the expectation that this will cause them to continue donating in the future once the incentive is removed).

9. Thanks to Peter Schuck for this insight. It may also be the case that my acting altruistically makes it less costly for another person to act altruistically. Thus personal altruism might help internalize the positive externalities of altruism in others, in effect subsidizing altruism with altruism.

10. *See infra* Section C.

11. Ronald H. Coase, *The Nature of the Firm*, 4 Econometrica 386 (1937).

12. *See id.* at 390.

13. *Id.* at 404–5.

14. *See* Armen A. Alchian & Harold Demsetz, *Production, Information Costs, and Economic Organization*, 62 Am. Econ. Rev. 777, 793, 795 (1972) (describing the firm as a "privately owned market" and downplaying the elements of command within firms); Bengt Holmstrom, *The Firm as a Subeconomy*, 15 J.L. Econ. & Org. 74 (1999); Oliver E. Williamson, *The Theory of the Firm as Governance Structure: From Choice to Contract*, 16 J. Econ. Perspectives 171 (2002).

15. *See, e.g.,* Robert N. Stavins & Bradley W. Whitehead, *The Next Generation of Market-Based Environmental Policies* (Environmental Reform: The Next Generation Project, Discussion Paper 97-10, Nov. 1996) (contrasting classic command-and-control environmental regulation with newer, mixed forms of state regulation that harness market forces); Yaa Akosa Antwi, Asoka S. Moriya, & Kosali Simon, *Effects of Federal Policy to Insure Young Adults: Evidence from the 2010 Affordable Care Act Dependent Coverage Mandate* (NBER Working Paper No. 18200, Dec. 2012) (describing the function of the Affordable Care Act, which commands individuals to buy health insurance while at the same time setting up markets and systems of subsidies to make such insurance more affordable).

16. The same was, of course, also true of merit goods. *See supra* Chapter 2, Section B.

17. *See* Alchian & Demsetz, *supra* note 14; Coase, *supra* note 11; Holmstrom, *supra* note 14; Martin Weitzman, *Prices vs. Quantities,* 41 Rev. Econ. Stud. 477 (1974); Williamson, *supra* note 14.

18. *See* Guido Calabresi & Philip Bobbitt, Tragic Choices 51–127 (1978) (discussing the use of modified command and modified markets to allocate tragic goods).

19. *See, e.g.,* Susan Rose-Ackerman, *Altruism, Nonprofits, and Economic Theory,* 34 J. Econ. Lit. 701, 710–18 (1996) (surveying the literature on models of altruism and theoretical accounts of the function of nonprofit organizations).

20. *See, e.g., HOPE Week: Helping Others Persevere & Excel,* New York Yankees (last visited Nov. 10, 2014), http://newyork.yankees.mlb.com/nyy/community/hope_index.jsp (describing "HOPE Week," during which the New York Yankees spend each day honoring an organization, individual, or family); Jon Pratt & Edson W. Spencer, *Dynamics of Corporate Philanthropy in Minnesota,* 129 Daedalus 269 (2000) (describing the Five Percent Club,

a group of large Minnesota corporations that committed to donating five percent of their earnings to philanthropy); Paul C. Godfrey, *The Relationship Between Corporate Philanthropy and Shareholder Wealth: A Risk Management Perspective*, 30 ACAD. MGMT. REV. 777 (2005) (arguing that corporate philanthropy is shareholder wealth–enhancing).

21. The source of this desire for altruism may be in our neural wiring and our evolutionary history as creatures that live in cooperative groups. *See* MATTHEW LIEBERMAN, SOCIAL: WHY OUR BRAINS ARE WIRED TO CONNECT (2013). But the full range of tastes in altruism is by no means confinable to a reductive evolutionary account. *See* PETER SINGER, THE EXPANDING CIRCLE: ETHICS, EVOLUTION, AND MORAL PROGRESS (1981) (arguing that our evolutionary sociobiology gave us the capacity for altruism, but that the full scope of specific altruistic behavior is a product of further factors like reason and culture).

22. *See* GREG O'BRIEN, A GUIDE TO NATURE ON CAPE COD AND THE ISLANDS 96 (1990) ("In coastal parts of the South during the 1700s and 1800s, lobsters were regularly fed to servants and slaves. There is a record of a group of Virginia indentured servants who, in the early 1700s, petitioned the colonial government that they 'should not be fed lobster more than twice a week.' The petition was granted in mercy.").

23. *Cf.* SINGER, *supra* note 21, at 3–22 (connecting humans' capacity for altruism to our deeply social nature: "Human beings are social animals. We were social before we were human."); LIEBERMAN, *supra* note 21 (drawing the same connection).

24. The same questions might also be asked concerning retribution and malevolence: How do we determine how much of these "bads" we want as a society? And are they better controlled through command or market structures? Malevolence is something we dislike. Retribution may be something we desire. We seem to have a taste for a very large amount of incarceration, and so we are willing to spend a great deal of resources for retribution against criminals. *See supra* Chapter 3, note 1.

25. *See* CALABRESI & BOBBITT, *supra* note 18, at 150–57; *supra* Chapter 4, Sections C–G.

26. The line between instrumental gifts and gifts as signs of affection is often subtle, but extremely important. It is self-defeating to try to purchase another's genuine love. But sexual favors are on occasion bought. The tax code seeks to distinguish bluntly between instrumental "gifts," which are taxed as income to the recipient, and noninstrumental ones that are instead subject to a gift tax on the donor. *See, e.g.,* United States v. Harris, 942 F.2d 1125, 1127 (7th Cir. 1991) (a case in which two sisters were charged with income tax evasion for not paying taxes on large sums of money provided by their lover; they

argued the payments were gifts). *See generally* Cosimo Mazzoni, The Gift Is the Tragedy (forthcoming) (analyzing the nature of gifts, and discussing their frequent self-serving characteristics).

27. *See* Leong, *supra* note 8.

28. *See, e.g.,* Charles T. Clotfelter, Federal Tax Policy and Charitable Giving (1985).

29. *See, e.g.,* Center on Philanthropy at Indiana University, The 2012 Bank of America Study of High Net Worth Philanthropy 71 (reporting the results of three surveys showing that if the charity tax deduction were eliminated, roughly 50 percent of wealthy households would not change their giving patterns and only 10 percent would "dramatically decrease" their giving); Jane G. Gravelle, Economic Analysis of the Charitable Contribution Deduction for Non-Itemizers, CRS Report RL31108, at 5–6 (2004) (showing that studies suggest charitable giving is price inelastic, and so not very responsive to tax changes).

30. *See* Leong, *supra* note 8.

31. *See* Center on Philanthropy, *supra* note 29; Gravelle, *supra* note 29; Leong, *supra* note 8.

32. *See* Pratt & Spencer, *supra* note 20.

33. *See* Joe Nocera, *Emerald City of Giving Does Exist,* N.Y. Times, Dec. 22, 2007.

34. With the decline of the rehabilitative model of criminal punishment, the criminal law is today seen—unfortunately from my point of view—as principally lowering crime by ensuring that "bad" people suppress their urges to commit crimes, or at least that "bad" people are kept in a place where they can commit no crimes, rather than convincing "bad" people to become morally "good." *But cf.* Jean Hampton, *The Moral Education Theory of Punishment,* 13 Phil. & Pub. Aff. 208 (1984) (expressing the idea that criminal punishment can morally uplift the criminal). Education, by contrast, is widely viewed as a tool to cultivate moral goodness because it does not directly *command* certain behavior to the recalcitrant, but instead teaches it to children.

35. *See* Barbara Nagy, *18 Connecticut Hospital Executives Earn More Than $1 Million,* New Haven Register, May 5, 2012.

36. *Cf.* Hirschman, *supra* note 3, at 52–53 (noting that economists and other social scientists have begun to take the complex varieties of human behavior seriously, and to abandon the attempt to categorize them all as variants of interest-motivated activity); *see also* David Grewal, Network Power: The Social Dynamics of Globalization (2009) (developing the concept of "network power" to explain the complex dynamics of globalization in a way applicable to individuals, governments, and market institutions).

37. We might here start by looking at the contributions of Alchian and Demsetz, and of Holmstrom, economists who, following Coase, have striven to blur the boundaries between pure markets and pure command structures. *See* Alchian & Demsetz, *supra* note 14; Holmstron, *supra* note 14.

38. Indeed, even markets and command institutions *themselves* have been viewed by distinguished scholars as valuable for their own sakes. *See infra* Chapter 6, Section C; *cf.* Coase, *supra* note 11, at 390 ("The price mechanism . . . might be superseded if the relationship which replaced it was desired for its own sake. This would be the case, for example, if some people preferred to work under the direction of some other person."); Friedrich A. Hayek, The Constitution of Liberty 21 (1960) ("Coercion is evil precisely because it . . . eliminates an individual as a thinking and valuing person and makes him a bare tool in the achievement of the ends of another."); Milton Friedman, Bright Promises, Dismal Performance 57 (1983) ("What we've really been talking about all along is freedom. Although a number of my proposals would have the immediate effect of improving our economic well-being, that's really a secondary goal to preserving individual freedom.").

39. *Compare* Martin Luther King, Jr., Nobel Prize Acceptance Speech (Dec. 10, 1964) ("After contemplation, I conclude that this award which I receive on behalf of that movement is a profound recognition that nonviolence is the answer to the crucial political and moral question of our time—the need for man to overcome oppression and violence without resorting to violence and oppression.") *with* Malcolm X, The Ballot or the Bullet (Mar. 8, 1964) ("I don't mean go out and get violent; but at the same time you should never be nonviolent unless you run into some nonviolence. I'm nonviolent with those who are nonviolent with me. But when you drop that violence on me, then you've made me go insane, and I'm not responsible for what I do."). For Martin Luther King, nonviolence was an end in itself—the ends of justice, as well as the means of achieving it, were both variables in his utility function. On the other hand, Malcolm X was indifferent among the means used to reach his desired ends, as powerfully expressed in his phrase "by any means necessary."

6
Of the Relationship of Markets and Command in the Liability Rule

1. Guido Calabresi & A. Douglas Melamed, *Property Rules, Liability Rules, and Inalienability: One View of the Cathedral,* 85 Harv. L. Rev. 1089 (1972).

2. *See, e.g.,* Abraham Bell & Gideon Parchomovsky, *Pliability Rules,* 101 MICH. L. REV. 1 (2002); Henry E. Smith, *Property and Property Rules,* 79 N.Y.U. L. REV. 1719, 1734 (2004) ("The prototypical example of liability rules comes from eminent domain."); Madeline Morris, *The Structure of Entitlements,* 78 CORNELL L. REV. 822 (1993). Of course, there has been another point of view. *See, e.g.,* JULES L. COLEMAN, RISKS AND WRONGS (1992); ERNEST J. WEIN-RIB, THE IDEA OF PRIVATE LAW (1995); John C. P. Goldberg & Benjamin C. Zipursky, *Torts as Wrongs,* 88 Tex. L. Rev. 917 (2010).

3. There are situations like eminent domain—or nuisance even—in which the person simply wishes to take someone else's entitlement. There are more situations in which the person wishes to engage in some activity, like running a bus company, which almost inevitably injures people and thereby has the effect, but not the aim, of taking their entitlements.

4. Guido Calabresi, *Torts—The Law of the Mixed Society,* 56 TEX. L. REV. 519, 521 (1978).

5. *See* Fred R. Shapiro & Michelle Pearse, *The Most-Cited Law Review Articles of All Time,* 110 MICH. L. REV. 1483, 1489 (2012). This description of "The Cathedral" as the most cited private law article has been made but, of course, depends on whether you treat Coase's "The Problem of Social Cost" as private or public. Many treat it as public. I myself treat it as private, and it is by far the most cited law review article of all time, public or private. *See* Shapiro & Pearse, *supra,* at 1489.

6. This literature is obviously too vast to cite in any detail. *See* Shapiro & Pearse, *supra* note 5, at 1489 (noting 1,980 citations to "The Cathedral").

7. Guido Calabresi, *A Broader View of the Cathedral: The Significance of the Liability Rule, Correcting a Misapprehension,* 77 LAW & CONTEMP. PROBS. 1 (2014).

8. The use of the word "price" as the assessment that is made collectively is misleading. It inevitably makes one think of a market. If one believes the collective decision to be an attempt to approach criminal law or regulation, the words that would most likely be used to describe the assessment are "penalty" or "sanction." *See* Robert Cooter, *Prices and Sanctions,* 84 COLUM. L. REV. 1523 (1984). If, finally, the charge made was intended to approach neither what a market would do nor what criminal law or regulation would impose, but a collective determination of how readily an entitlement should shift, then a word like "assessment" would seem appropriate. Because the literature about liability rules has used the word "price" almost exclusively, I continue frequently to use that word, but I wish to emphasize how problematic that use really is. I am grateful to Greg Keating for this and many other useful suggestions.

9. This Section is taken almost directly, with permission, from Calabresi, *supra* note 7, at 7–12.

10. *See* A. Mitchell Polinsky & Steven Shavell, *Punitive Damages: An Economic Analysis*, 111 HARV. L. REV. 869, 887–96 (1998); Catherine M. Sharkey, *Punitive Damages as Societal Damages*, 113 YALE L.J. 347, 363–72 (2003); *cf.* Ciraolo v. City of New York, 216 F.3d 236, 245 (2d Cir. 2000) (Calabresi, J., concurring) ("Such a [multiplier] conception of damages . . . is not new."); *Kemezy v. Peters*, 79 F.3d 33, 35 (7th Cir. 1996) (Posner, J.) (offering a deterrence rationale for punitive damages); Guido Calabresi, *The Complexity of Torts—The Case of Punitive Damages, in* EXPLORING TORT LAW 333 (M. Stuart Madden ed., 2005). Of course, some of these writers also suggested, at least in passing, that there might be more to punitive damages than mimicking the market. *See, e.g.,* Sharkey, *supra,* at 362–63 n.41, 369 n.56 (noting other uses of punitive damages).

11. W. Kip Viscusi, *Jurors, Judges, and the Mistreatment of Risk by the Courts*, 30 J. LEGAL STUD. 107, 111–15 (2001).

12. *See infra* Section C; *see also* Ward Farnsworth, *Do Parties to Nuisance Cases Bargain After Judgment? A Glimpse Inside the Cathedral*, 66 U. CHI. L. REV. 373, 379 (1999); Benjamin Shmueli, *What Have Calabresi & Melamed Got to Do with Family Affairs? Women Using Tort Law in Order to Defeat Jewish and Shari'a Law*, 25 BERKELEY J. GENDER L. & JUST. 125, 148–55 (2010) [hereinafter Shmueli, *Family Affairs*]; Benjamin Shmueli, *When Can Post-Judgment Bargaining Succeed? Another Glimpse at the Cathedral* (Aug. 16, 2014) (unpublished manuscript) (on file with the author) [hereinafter Shmueli, *Post-Judgment Bargaining*].

13. *See* DAN B. DOBBS, THE LAW OF TORTS § 302 (2000) (discussing emotional harm); Anita Bernstein, *Keep It Simple: An Explanation of the Role of No Recovery for Pure Economic Loss*, 48 ARIZ. L. REV. 773 (2006).

14. *See* GUIDO CALABRESI, IDEALS, BELIEFS, ATTITUDES, AND THE LAW: PRIVATE LAW PERSPECTIVES ON A PUBLIC LAW PROBLEM 72–76 (1985).

15. *Id.* at 77–78.

16. Morton Horwitz famously argued that nineteenth-century tort law amounted to a subsidy in support of industrialization. *See* MORTON J. HORWITZ, THE TRANSFORMATION OF AMERICAN LAW, 1780–1860, at 63–108 (1977); *cf.* Robert L. Rabin, *The Historical Development of the Fault Principle: A Reinterpretation*, 15 GA. L. REV. 925 (1981) (arguing that the nineteenth century was not entirely a "fault" century but in significant aspects a nonfault century during which rules like the fellow–servant rule were employed to favor defendants). Some also argue that developing countries often have liability rules that are "low priced" in comparison to developed countries in order to spur

industrialization and economic competitiveness. *See, e.g.,* Jack L. Goldsmith & Alan O. Sykes, Lex Loci Delictus *and Global Economic Welfare:* Spinozzi v. ITT Sheraton Corp., 120 Harv. L. Rev. 1137, 1137–42 (2007) (discussing Judge Posner's economic account of the choice-of-law rule *lex loci delicti commissi*).

17. *See, e.g.,* Wal-Mart Stores, Inc. v. Dukes, 131 S. Ct. 2541 (2011); AT&T Mobility L.L.C. v. Concepcion, 131 S. Ct. 1740 (2011).

18. Although the lion's share of attention to "The Cathedral" has been devoted to property and liability rules, Melamed and I there explicitly discussed this third category, which we called "inalienability rules." *See* Calabresi & Melamed, *supra* note 1, at 1111–15; *see also* Susan Rose-Ackerman, *Inalienability and the Theory of Property Rights,* 85 Colum. L. Rev. 931 (1985); Lee Anne Fennell, *Adjusting Alienability,* 122 Harv. L. Rev. 1403, 1443 (2009).

19. *See* Giuseppe Franco Ferrari, *Fundamental Rights and Freedoms, in* Introduction to Italian Public Law 255, 271–72 (Giuseppe Franco Ferrari ed., 2008) (discussing the divergence between market value and compensation paid in Italian cases of expropriation).

20. *See* Kelo v. City of New London, 545 U.S. 469 (2005).

21. *Id.* at 489–90.

22. *See* David de Sola, *Souter's Home an Activist Target,* CNN (Jan. 22, 2006, 11:39 a.m.), http://www.cnn.com/2006/LAW/01/21/eminent.domain.

23. Oral Argument at 21:48, *Kelo,* 545 U.S. 469 (No. 04-108), *available at* http://www.oyez.org/cases/2000-2009/2004/2004_04_108 ("Are there any writings . . . that indicate[] that when you have property being taken from one private person ultimately to go to another private person, that what we ought to do is to adjust the measure of compensation, so that the owner . . . can receive some sort of a premium for the development?").

24. For interesting and very recent discussions of this question, see Lee Anne Fennell, *Just Enough,* 113 Colum. L. Rev. Sidebar 109 (2013); Brian Angelo, *Just Undercompensation: The Idiosyncratic Premium in Eminent Domain,* 113 Colum. L. Rev. 593 (2013); and Shmueli, *Post-Judgment Bargaining, supra* note 12.

25. This kind of thing happened even in the nineteenth century. *See, e.g.,* Richard A. Epstein, Takings: Private Property and the Power of Eminent Domain 170–75 (1985) (discussing Mill Acts that required those who flooded neighboring lands to pay above-market prices to the owners of the land damaged).

26. *See* Rylands v. Fletcher [1868], 3 L.R.E. & I. App. 330 (H.L.) 338–39 (appeal taken from Eng.); *see also* Horwitz, *supra* note 16 (discussing the rise of negligence); Rabin, *supra* note 16 (highlighting the complexity of

nineteenth-century tort doctrine). While the doctrines discussed by Horwitz are described by him as representing a subsidy for industry, *Rylands,* like the Mill Acts, could be viewed as effectuating a tax.

27. The liability rule may become even more of an instrument of both collectivist and libertarian choice elements in the future. *Cf.* Ugo Mattei & Fernanda Nicola, *A "Social Dimension" in European Private Law? The Call for Setting a Progressive Agenda,* 41 NEW ENG. L. REV. 1 (2006). In various conference papers, Mattei has also remarked the interesting asymmetry between the application of a liability rule in the case of eminent domain, where the owner of private property is compensated at a collectively set rate when that property is taken for public use, and the absence of such a rule in the case of privatization, where members of the public are not compensated for the particular cost to them that privatization causes. *Cf.* Saki Bailey & Ugo Mattei, *Social Movements as Constituent Power: The Italian Struggle for the Commons,* 20 IND. J. GLOBAL LEGAL STUD. 965, 990 (2013).

28. *See* Rose-Ackerman, *supra* note 18.

29. *See* Calabresi, *supra* note 7; *see also* Shmueli, *Family Affairs, supra* note 12, at 148–55; Shmueli, *Post-Judgment Bargaining, supra* note 12.

30. R. H. Coase, *The Nature of the Firm,* 4 ECONOMICA 386 (1937).

31. Like Coase, some other great economists have seen this dual function in particular contexts. *See, e.g.,* Amartya Sen, *Development as Capability Expansion, in* THE COMMUNITY DEVELOPMENT READER 319 (James Defillipis & Susan Saegert eds., 2012); Paul Streeten, *Human Development: Means and Ends,* 84 AM. ECON. REV. 232 (1994) (treating human development and the eradication of poverty as both good in themselves and instrumental for a variety of other ends, such as higher productivity). I have not myself, however, seen a generalized treatment of this very important attribute that many goods share to some extent and some in dramatic fashion. For further discussion, see my essays in the present book on altruism and on tastes and values, *supra* Chapter 4 and *infra* Chapters 7 and 8.

32. Admittedly, this view of markets as intrinsically good is more readily seen in libertarians' description of command as an intrinsic evil. *See supra* Chapter 5, note 38.

33. *See, e.g.,* Armen A. Alchian & Harold Demsetz, *Production, Information Costs, and Economic Organization,* 62 AM. ECON. REV. 777 (1972); OLIVER E. WILLIAMSON, MARKETS AND HIERARCHIES: ANALYSIS AND ANTITRUST IMPLICATIONS (1975).

34. *See, e.g.,* Ian Ayres & Eric Talley, *Solomonic Bargaining: Dividing a Legal Entitlement to Facilitate Coasean Trade,* 104 YALE L.J. 1027 (1995); Ian Ayres & Eric Talley, *Distinguishing Between Consensual and Nonconsensual*

Advantages of Liability Rules, 105 YALE L.J. 235, 242–43 (1995); Louis Kaplow & Steven Shavell, *Property Rules Versus Liability Rules: An Economic Analysis,* 109 HARV. L. REV. 713, 718 (1996); Daphna Lewinsohn-Zamir, *The Choice Between Property Rules and Liability Rules Revisited: Critical Observations from Behavioral Studies,* 80 TEX. L. REV. 219 (2001); Ian Ayres & Paul M. Goldbart, *Correlated Values in the Theory of Property and Liability Rules,* 32 J. LEGAL STUD. 121, 126 (2003).

35. Treble damages have given rise to a whole literature on enforcement through private attorneys general. *See, e.g.,* Kenneth Mann, *Punitive Civil Sanctions: The Middleground Between Criminal and Civil Law,* 101 YALE L.J. 1795, 1865 (1992) ("[P]unitive civil sanctions play a central role in protecting society from both underenforcement and overenforcement of the norms that make up the social order."); Norman Abrams, *A New Proposal for Limiting Private Civil RICO,* 37 UCLA L. REV. 1, 7 (1989) ("[T]he primary rationale for the private attorney general model [is] to provide additional resources to supplement public prosecution."). The Supreme Court has also noted this prevailing rationale for treble damages in both the civil RICO and antitrust contexts. *See* Sedima, S.P.R.L. v. Imrex Co., 473 U.S. 479, 493 (1985) ("Private attorney general provisions such as § 1964(c) are in part designed to fill prosecutorial gaps."); Reiter v. Sonotone Corp., 442 U.S. 330, 344 (1979) ("These private suits provide a significant supplement to the limited resources available to the Department of Justice for enforcing the antitrust laws and deterring violations.").

36. *See* Shmueli, *Family Affairs, supra* note 12, at 148–55; Shmueli, *Post-Judgment Bargaining, supra* note 12.

37. *See* Rose-Ackerman, *supra* note 18.

7
Of Tastes and Values Ignored

1. One can—and perhaps should in many situations—distinguish between tastes and values. *See, e.g.,* Robert Cooter, *Do Good Laws Make Good Citizens?: An Economic Analysis of Internalized Norms,* 86 VA. L. REV. 1577 (2000); Gregory C. Keating, *Pricelessness and Life: An Essay for Guido Calabresi,* 64 MD. L. REV. 159 (2005). For instance, Elizabeth Anderson differentiates tastes and values on the basis that the latter represent not mere likings or preferences, about which there is no rational dispute, but ways of ranking or ordering (or, if you like, "preferring") that entail various modes of justification. *See* ELIZABETH ANDERSON, VALUES IN ETHICS AND ECONOMICS

(1995). Daniel Hausman, in contrast, sees the two not as distinct conceptions of preference but as factors responsible for a person's total comparative evaluation or "all-things-considered" ranking. *See* Daniel Hausman, *Sympathy, Commitment, and Preference,* 21 ECON. & PHIL. 33 (2005). I choose not to differentiate between tastes and values here because I believe that what I have to say applies equally to each of the myriad definitions that are given to these terms in law and in economics.

2. In his article arguing that juries err in myriad ways, Viscusi suggests that punitive damage awards are irrational when the dollar-denominated value of damaged luggage is less than the cost of the repair that would have prevented the luggage damage. *See* W. Kip Viscusi, *Jurors, Judges, and the Mistreatment of Risk by the Courts,* 30 J. LEGAL STUD. 107, 111–15 (2001). I do not dispute that luggage may well not be worth the protection that Viscusi's survey participants sought to give it, but to assume this based on dollar values is to overlook the private value that people often place on their possessions.

3. Guido Calabresi & A. Douglas Melamed, *Property Rules, Liability Rules, and Inalienability: One View of the Cathedral,* 85 HARV. L. REV. 1089 (1972). Indeed, I may love my luggage more than I love Ronald Coase—unlikely, but possible. If that is so, I may seek property rule protection for that beloved luggage. And, as discussed in Chapter 6, *supra,* punitive damages can approximate such protection.

4. That people tend to give greater weight to the vastly different values given to life and body parts than to those given to property is fairly clear. For example, individuals have an unlimited insurance interest in life, but not in property. *See, e.g.,* Ala. Code § 27-14-3 ("An individual has an unlimited insurable interest in his or her own life, health, and bodily safety."). This represents a collective judgment on the relative merits of one set of values versus the other. And, of course, such collective judgments are part of our legal system. Indeed, in Chapter 8, I will argue that they should be considered by economists as well. But so long as one considers tastes and values to be a matter of individual decision only, one cannot distinguish between luggage-lovers and kidney-lovers.

5. *See generally,* W. KIP VISCUSI, FATAL TRADEOFFS (1992); W. Kip Viscusi, *The Value of Risks to Life and Health,* 31 J. ECON. LIT. 1912 (1993).

6. Guido Calabresi, *The Pointlessness of Pareto: Carrying Coase Further,* 100 YALE L.J. 1211 (1991). For example, one reason people may fail to make agreements that would otherwise make them better off in some material way is anger at the other party. *See* Ward Farnsworth, *Do Parties to Nuisance Cases Bargain After Judgment? A Glimpse Inside the Cathedral,* 66 U. CHI. L. REV. 373, 421 (1999) (examining twenty nuisance cases and showing that

no bargaining took place after judgment, primarily because of animosity between the parties). *See also* Daphna Lewinson-Zamir, *Do the Right Thing: Indirect Remedies in Private Law*, 94 B.U. L. REV. 55, 85–88 (2014) (advocating "indirect remedies" to resolve contract disputes in part because they reduce expressive and nonmonetary harms, such as hostility).

7. Modern microeconomics has evolved over the twentieth century from its neoclassical roots and is now "much better defined by its eclectic formalistic modeling approach than by its beliefs." HARRY LANDRETH & DAVID C. COLANDER, HISTORY OF ECONOMIC THOUGHT 419 (4th ed., 2001). The increasing reliance on modeling that has come to dominate the profession grew out of the formalist revolution of the 1930s, 1940s, and 1950s, *id.* at 401–19, and was, for example, prominently advanced in the subsequent decades by work done in such distinguished places as the graduate department in economics at MIT and the Cowles Foundation for Research in Economics at Yale.

8. This has been especially true in the field of political science, where, as a result of the legitimation of mathematical modeling in economics, "the incentive structure . . . began to encourage an orientation modeled on the physical sciences. The pressure for conformity can be measured in terms of prestige, journal publications, fellowships and grants. . . . Projects that have the appearance of hard science have had the inside track for gaining substantive research support." GABRIEL A. ALMOND, A DISCIPLINE DIVIDED: SCHOOLS AND SECTS IN POLITICAL SCIENCE 46 (1990). The dominance of quantitative methods has also been reflected in many graduate programs in political science, such that "[p]olitical theory and philosophy, public law and public administration, and descriptive institutional analysis have all become defensive, peripheral, and secondary subject matters." *Id.*

9. To mention but one classic, consider the wonderful debate between Richard Titmuss and Kenneth Arrow on the effect of selling blood on blood donations. *See supra* Chapter 3, note 7. *See also* Albert O. Hirschman, *The Concept of Interest: From Euphemism to Tautology, in* RIVAL VIEWS OF MARKET SOCIETY AND OTHER RECENT ESSAYS 35–55 (1986), and the sources cited therein. My object here, however, is to focus on one aspect of the topic in order to make a point about tastes and values that, I believe, has not been sufficiently emphasized in that literature.

10. *See e.g.,* O. E. WILLIAMSON, MARKET AND HIERARCHIES: ANALYSIS AND ANTITRUST IMPLICATIONS (1975); Oliver Hart & John Moore, *Property Rights and the Nature of the Firm*, 98 J. POL. ECON. 1119 (1990); Sanford J. Grossman & Oliver D. Hart, *The Costs and Benefits of Ownership: A Theory of Vertical and Lateral Integration*, 94 J. POL. ECON. 691 (1986); O. E. Williamson,

Markets and Hierarchies: Some Elementary Considerations, 63 Am. Econ. Rev. 316 (1973).

11. *See, e.g.,* Louis Kaplow & Steven Shavell, *The Conflict Between Notions of Fairness and the Pareto Principle,* 6 Am. L. & Econ. Rev. 63, 64 (1999); Louis Kaplow & Steven Shavell, *Why the Legal System Is Less Efficient than the Income Tax in Redistributing Income,* 23 J. Legal Stud. 667, 677 (1994).

12. The same, of course, is also the case with respect to not a few garden variety external costs: some may be corrected through market behavior, thus some individuals may, if they are bothered enough, seek to diminish such externalities by making voluntary payments. But often, too, collective action is taken to eliminate or reduce the externalities. Simple examples are housing codes that require the use of certain fire retardant building materials. *See, e.g.,* Cal. Building Code Ch. 7A (Jan. 2009 Supp.) (requiring "ignition proof" materials for any new construction in certain areas at risk of wild fires). In this sense, there is no difference between "typical" externalities and the moral externalities I am discussing here.

13. For a description of the Kaldor-Hicks test, *see infra* note 20. *See also infra* Section B.3.

14. *See, e.g.,* Jones v. Mayer Co., 392 U.S. 409 (1968); Shelley v. Kraemer 334 U.S. 1 (1948). *See also* 42 U.S.C. § 1982 (2012) ("All citizens of the United States shall have the same right, in every State and Territory, as is enjoyed by white citizens thereof to inherit, purchase, lease, sell, hold, and convey real and personal property.").

15. *See supra* Chapter 3, note 9.

16. For a detailed historic account of the various approaches taken to military conscription in the United States, *see* Guido Calabresi & Phillip Bobbitt, Tragic Choices 158–67 (1978).

17. In the United States, for example, the sale of organs (and by extension other body parts) is prohibited by federal law. *See* National Organ Transplant Act, 42 U.S.C. §§ 273–74g (2012). As of 2009, ninety-one nations had specific legislation governing organ transplants and donations. United Nations & Council of Eur., Trafficking in Organs, Tissues and Cells and Trafficking in Human Beings for the Purpose of the Removal of Organs 47 (2009).

18. Economic models generally assume simple wealth maximization, though some economists have incorporated interdependent utility functions into their models. *See supra* Chapter 2, note 11.

19. Calabresi, *supra* note 6.

20. A change in allocation is Kaldor-Hicks efficient if at least one party benefits from the move to it, and any party that is harmed by the change

could, in theory, be compensated for the harm by the party or parties that have benefited from it. *See* John Hicks, *The Foundations of Welfare Economics,* 49 ECON. J. 696 (1939); Nicholas Kaldor, *Welfare Propositions in Economics and Interpersonal Comparisons of Utility,* 49 ECON. J. 549 (1939).

21. Calabresi, *supra* note 6 at 1216–21, 1230–31.

22. *See supra* Chapter 1, Section C.

23. As I define the term, a limited war is one in which it is much safer to remain at home than to join the army. For a more detailed discussion of the problems with a volunteer army in a limited war, *see* CALABRESI & BOBBITT, *supra* note 16, 125–26.

24. What I say in this chapter and the next is adapted from a lecture I gave at the annual meeting of the American Law and Economics Association at Stanford Law School on May 18, 2012, upon receiving the Ronald H. Coase Medal. That lecture was subsequently published by the American Law and Economics Review. Guido Calabresi, *Of Tastes and Values,* 16 AM. L. & ECON. REV. 313 (2014).

8
Of Tastes and Values

1. Brown v. Bd. of Ed., 347 U.S. 483 (1954); Plessy v. Ferguson, 63 U.S. 537 (1896). For a discussion of *Brown*'s effect on attitudes toward race, *see, e.g.,* David Garrow, *Hopelessly Hollow History: Revisionist Devaluing of* Brown v. Board of Education, 80 VA. L. REV. 151 (1994).

2. Goodridge v. Dept. of Public Health, 440 Mass. 309 (2003).

3. *See* Jesse Wegman, *Why Massachusetts Led the Way on Same-Sex Marriage,* N.Y. TIMES, April 27, 2015, at A18 (describing the initial legislative backlash against same-sex marriage, and the subsequent rapid shift in public opinion toward favoring it).

4. Roe v. Wade, 410 U.S. 113 (1973). For example, Neal Devins has argued that *Roe v. Wade* created a backlash and a change in values that increased the opposition to abortion. Neal Devins, *I Love You Big Brother,* 87 CAL. L. REV. 1283 (1999). On the other hand, it is hard to deny that since *Roe v. Wade* abortions have become more common and more accepted by many people. Notably, Robert Post and Reva Siegel have argued that the reaction to *Roe v. Wade* is far more complicated than the initial narrative suggested. *See* Robert Post & Reva Siegel, Roe *Rage: Democratic Constitutionalism and Backlash,* 42 HARV. C.R.-C.L. L. REV. 373 (2008). In particular, while *Roe*'s opponents certainly did mobilize against the opinion and the values it stood

for, attributing those oppositional forces to the opinion itself is by no means easy. *Id.* at 406–30.

5. Dred Scott v. Sandford, 60 U.S. 393 (1857).

6. *See, e.g.,* ERIC FONER, FREE SOIL, FREE LABOR, FREE MEN: THE IDEOLOGY OF THE REPUBLICAN PARTY BEFORE THE CIVIL WAR 97–101, 209 (1995) (describing Republican adoption only after *Dred Scott* of the argument that the southern "Slave Power" would spread slavery to the North and noting that the decision "convinced many moderates that radical claims regarding the Slave Power's intentions were fully justified").

7. In chapter 3 of my book, I listed the primary goals of accident law and in doing so said nothing on accident law's role in shaping taste and values. *See* GUIDO CALABRESI, THE COSTS OF ACCIDENTS: A LEGAL AND ECONOMIC ANALYSIS 24 (1970). The end of the chapter included a brief section on "other goals" outside of accident law, but even there I paid scant attention to tastes and values, concluding that "there is little point in discussing outside goals in the abstract." *Id.* at 33. For criticism of this oversight in my early work, *see, e.g.,* Mark Kelman, *Misunderstanding Social Life: A Critique of the Core Premises of "Law and Economics,"* 33 J. LEG. ED. 274 (1983).

8. *See, e.g.,* CALABRESI, *supra* note 7; GUIDO CALABRESI, IDEALS, BELIEFS, ATTITUDES, AND THE LAW: PRIVATE LAW PERSPECTIVES ON A PUBLIC LAW PROBLEM (1985); Guido Calabresi, *The Decision for Accidents: An Approach to Non-Fault Allocation of Costs,* 78 HARV. L. REV. 713, 713 (1965).

9. *See, e.g.,* Guido Calabresi, *Toward a Unified Theory of Torts,* 1 J. TORT L. 1932 (2007).

10. *See, e.g.,* Genesis 1:26–27.

11. In some ways, however, women in the upper classes of very hierarchical and class-conscious societies fared better than women in more egalitarian (in terms of wealth) cultures. Thus, for example, there were great female scholars and academics in the upper classes in Italy during the Renaissance and through the Enlightenment. Laura Bassi comes immediately to mind. Born into a wealthy Bolognese family in 1711 (her father was a lawyer), Bassi became the first female professor in Europe at the age of twenty when she was given a teaching position at the University of Bologna after being awarded a doctorate in physics. *See* EUROPEAN COMMISSION, WOMEN IN SCIENCE 38–41 (2009). In 1738 she married a fellow academic and went on to have a distinguished and productive scientific career. *Id.* She is also reported to have borne twelve children. As Londa Schiebinger notes, it is likely that Bassi's accomplishments were made possible because of the different attitudes toward child rearing in the Italian upper class at the time: "In the Eighteenth-Century, the child was handed over soon after birth to a governess or wet nurse and

reared in the countryside. A mother might not see the child again until age seven—about the time boys were sent away to boarding school. . . . [The] prerogatives of class [thus] allowed Bassi to be both scientist and mother." Londa Schiebinger, *Women in Science: Historical Perspectives,* Address at the Space Telescope Science Institute (Sept. 8, 1992), *in* Women at Work: A Meeting on the Status of Women in Astronomy at 13, *available at* http://www.stsci. edu/institute/conference/wia/.

12. Equality has, indeed, been most readily granted (both for racial and ethnic minorities and for women) only insofar as the minority group agrees to assimilation. *See, e.g.,* Catharine A. MacKinnon, *Reflections on Sex Equality Under Law,* 100 YALE L.J. 1281, 1288 (1991) ("The essentially assimilationist approach fundamental to [the] legal equality doctrine—be like us and we will treat you like we treat each other—was adopted in sex cases wholesale from the cases on racial discrimination."). The result is that groups seeking equality are often presented with what Martha Minow has referred to as the "difference dilemma":

> This nation is committed to both pluralism and equality, yet it also bears a history of prejudice against people whom the dominant group calls different. Indeed, differences in race, gender, and ethnicity have spelled determinate positions on its social hierarchy. But nonrecognition of difference leaves in place a faulty neutrality, constructed so as to advance the dominant group and hinder those who are different. . . . Identification or acknowledgment of a trait of difference, associated by the dominant group with minority identity, risks recreating occasions for majority discrimination based on that trait. Nonidentification or nonacknowledgment, however, risks recreating occasions for discrimination based on majority practices, such as tests, norms, and judgments forged without regard for difference, or with regard solely for the perspective, needs, and interests of the dominant group.

Martha Minow, *Learning to Live with the Dilemma of Difference: Bilingual and Special Education,* 48 LAW & CONTEMP. PROBS. 158, 159–60 (1985). *See also* KENJI YOSHINO, COVERING: THE HIDDEN ASSAULT ON OUR CIVIL RIGHTS (2006).

13. An argument can, of course, always be made that when professionals do something well (and perhaps better than any individual could do it), it is better to let them do so, even though it removes highly creative work from individuals. Numerous states, including most recently New York,

have, at least in part, agreed with this argument in deciding to offer universal prekindergarten. It remains an open question whether prekindergarten in fact provides lasting advantages to children. *See* Will Boisevert, *It's a Boon for Politicians and Parents, But Does Universal Pre-K Really Help Kids?*, N.Y. Observer, Sept. 4, 2014 (reviewing debate among researchers on long-term effectiveness of pre-k programs). But even if it does, adopting the professional alternative comes at a cost, and it is the recognition and evaluation of that cost that is my object here.

14. It does raise again, however, the possible utility of modified markets, whereby society would seek to increase altruism and bestow greater status on those who care for children using indirect, money-like transfers rather than direct cash payments. *See supra* Chapter 5, Sections D–G.

15. *See, e.g.,* Adam Smith, Lectures on Jurisprudence (R. L. Meek, D. D. Raphael, & Peter Stein eds., 1976); Friedrich A. Hayek, *The Atavism of Social Justice, in* New Studies in Philosophy, Politics, Economics, and the History of Ideas (1978); *supra* Chapter 5, note 38.

16. *See supra* Chapter 1, Section C.

17. Thus the great German legal scholar Konrad Zweigert greeted my presentation of the New Economic Analysis of Law, at a seminar at the Max Planck Institute in Hamburg in 1965, with the categorical statement: "That is all very interesting, but you must realize that it isn't law or legal scholarship." My rather rude answer, "Perhaps not now, but it soon will be," was all too prescient.

Index

Printed and bound by CPI Group (UK) Ltd, Croydon, CR0 4YY

02/01/2025

14619421-0001